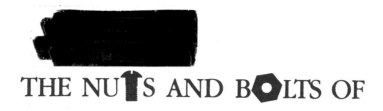

THE NUTS AND BOLTS OF

CAREER COUNSELING:

HOW TO SET UP & SUCCEED IN PRIVATE PRACTICE

Edited by

Al A. Hafer

Career Counselor Services, Inc.
Greenville, SC

National Career Development Association

This is one of a series of booklets sponsored by the National Career Development Association and published jointly with the Garrett Park Press. The titles published to date are as follows:

Counseling Midlife Career Changers by Loretta Bradley

Designing and Implementing a Career Information Center by Sandra Thompson Brown and Duane Brown

The Nuts and Bolts of Career Counseling: How to Set up and Succeed in Private Practice edited by Al A. Hafer

Library of Congress Cataloging-in-Publication Data

The Nuts and bolts of career counseling : how to set up & succeed in
  private practice / edited by Al A. Hafer.
      p.   cm.
   Includes bibliographical references.
   ISBN 0-912048-97-2
   1. Vocational guidance. 2. Professions--Marketing. 3. Employee
counseling--Vocational guidance.   I. Hafer, Al A.
HF5381.N88   1992
153.6'068--dc20
                                                            91-40632
                                                            CIP

Published and distributed by the Garrett Park Press
PO Box 190
Garrett Park, MD 20896

TABLE OF CONTENTS

LIST OF FIGURES

About the authors . . .

Chapter One — Al A. Hafer, NCCC, NCC, LPC, has been Executive Director of Career Counselor Services, Inc. of Greenville, SC since 1983. He has been Trustee at Large for the NCDA, Co-Chair of the NCDA Career Counseling in Private Practice SIG, and President of the South Carolina Career Development Association. Prior to establishing his own private practice Dr. Hafer had 30 years of management experience in the General Electric Co.

Chapter Two — Edwin L. Herr, NCCC, NCC, is Professor and Head, Division of Counseling and Educational Psychology and Career Studies at the Pennsylvania State University in University Park, PA. He is also a partner in Career Counseling, Consultation and Assessment Associates. Dr. Herr is a past President of NCDA, past President of the National Vocational Guidance Association, past President of the Association for Counselor Education and Supervision and a Fellow of the American Psychological Association. He has authored/coauthored more than 200 articles, reviews and book chapters and 28 books on career counseling, vocational education and counseling.

Chapter Three — Norma K. Zuber, NCCC, NCC, has been President of Career and Life Planning, Norma Zuber & Associates, in Ventura, CA since 1987. She has been a member of the Board of Directors of the California Career Development Association and Chairperson of the Legislative Task Force special project related to licensing of professional career counselors in private practice in California. She has also taught career development and career transition classes at several colleges.

Chapter Four — Mary-Lynne Musgrove, NCCC, NCC, LPC, is President of Musgrove Career Counseling in Columbus, OH. She has had 21 years experience in career counseling, ten of which have been in private practice. She has made a number of presentations on career counseling and was co-editor of a book on adult career counseling. She has a particular interest in mid-career change and the psychological aspects of career counseling.

Chapter Five — Diane Shepard, NCCC, NCC, RPC, is an Assistant Professor, Department of Human Services at the University of North Carolina at Charlotte, NC and President of the Career Center, her private practice. Dr. Shepard is co-chair of the NCDA Career Counselors in Private Practice SIG, past President of the North Carolina Career Development Association and is President of the North Carolina Association for Counseling and Development. She is involved in business consulting and training for a number of national companies. She has been a speaker on many radio and TV talk shows to discuss career development topics.

Chapter Six — Michael Shahnasarian, NCCC, NCC, CVE, CRC, LMHC, has been President of Career Consultants of America, Inc. of Tampa, FL since 1985. He is Chairperson of the NCDA Career Development in Business and Indusry SIG and President of the Suncoast Chapter of the American Society for Training and Development. He has authored and coauthored 18 articles (many on computer-assisted career guidance systems), has conducted professional training and has made 11 presentations at professional conventions and conferences. He has also appeared on Tampa area radio and TV stations discussing the area labor market.

Chapter Seven — Frank S. Karpati, NCCC, NCC, CC, has been Executive Director of Career Directions in Hackensack, NJ since 1977. He has been on the Board of Directors of NCDA and the New Jersey Professional Counselor Association and past President of the New Jersey Career Counselor Association. He was instrumental in developing NCDA's position statement on National Certified Career Counselors (NCCC). He has contributed to numerous professional publications, co-authored books, conducted research, appeared on radio and TV programs and addressed national professional gatherings.

ACRONYMS

AACD — American Association for Counseling and Development

ACCI — Adult Career Concerns Inventory

A.I. — Assessment Instrument

All — Ethics codes from AACD, NBCC, NCDA and SCLPC all apply

B.A. — Bachelor of Arts

CACG — Computer-assisted career guidance system

CC — Certified Counselor

CCA — Career Consultants of America, Inc.

CRC — Certified Rehabilitation Counselor

CVE — Certified Vocational Expert

DOT — *Dictionary of Occupational Titles* (see Appendix)

LMHC — Licensed Mental Health Counselor

LPC — Licensed Professional Counselor

MBTI — Myers-Briggs Type Indicator

NBCC — National Board for Certified Counselors

NCC — National Certified Counselor

NCCC — National Certified Career Counselor

NCDA — National Career Development Association

RPC — Registered Professional Counselor

SDS — Self-Directed Search

SCLPC — South Carolina Licensed Professional Counselor

SIG — Special Interest Group

SII — Strong Interest Inventory

PREFACE

The Board of Directors of the National Career Development Association (NCDA) decided in 1989 that it was timely to sponsor a Professional Development Institute for career counseling in private practice. Co-chairs of its Career Counseling in Private Practice Special Interest Group, Al Hafer and Frank Karpati, were asked in 1990 to organize and put on a Pre-Convention Workshop for the American Association for Counseling and Development. This all day workshop was entitled *The Nuts and Bolts of Private Practice Career Counseling* and featured seven career counselors experienced in private practice. Two of the seven had as their primary place of employment a university setting, plus a private practice on the side. The other five counselors were full time in private practice.

The workshop had as its objective providing the latest thinking on private practice career counseling to those who were already in full-time private practice, as well as to career counselors conducting private practice.

After the workshop was conducted so many requests from those in private practice or considering it were received for written materials that this book was prepared. The authors express appreciation to the Media Committee, chaired by Dr. Arnold Spokane, who made a number of constructive suggestions improving on the initial manuscript. We also appreciate the support of the Board of Directors of NCDA for publication of the material included in this book.

Al A. Hafer

Greenville, SC
Janaury 1992

Chapter One — Introducton, Potential Private Practice Problems and Ethics

Al A. Hafer
Career Counselor Services, Inc.
Greenville, SC

Career counseling has made significant progress in both theory and application since Frank Parsons' work in the early 1900s (Montross & Shinkman, 1981). The National Career Development Association, the oldest counseling association in the United States (founded in 1913), has continued to play a leading role in the development of career counseling. The NCDA has conducted many content sessions and workshops to assist professional career counselors in improving career counseling skills. In addition it publishes the *Career Development Quarterly,* a newsletter and has published many books on career counseling, several of the recent ones being Kapes & Mastie (1988), Leibowitz & Lea (1986), Brown & Minor (1989), Brown & Brown (1990), and Bradley (1990).

Recently the NCDA has instituted a new series of career counseling "How to Do It" books in cooperation with the Garrett Park Press. These books are designed to inform and help professional career counselors assist clients in career development. Two prior books in this new series have been authored by Bradley (1990) and Brown and Brown (1990). This book is another of the "How to Do It" series.

Potential Private Practice Problems

The NCDA Media Committee suggested that this book discuss frequently encountered private practice problems. This section covers problems that may be encountered during the start up of a private practice, as well as problems that may be encountered in established lished enterprises.

Referrals — Career counselors in private practice encounter clients with a broad range of problems. The counselor needs to decide what problems he or she should handle and what, if any, should be referred and appropriate referral sources. In reverse, many clients have been referred to me for career counseling by psychotherapists and psychologists. Ed Herr discusses this subject in more detail in Chapter Two.

Client Intake System — In Chapter Three Norma Zuber presents excellent coverage of this important topic. If you are already in private practice you should review this material to see if your current intake system could be improved.

Special Problems Encountered in Outplacement Counseling — When an individual has lost a job with a company after 30 years it is a very traumatic experience which causes depression, lowers self esteem and may cause very bizarre behavior. Outplacement counseling frequently involves the same six emotional stages described by Kubler-Ross (1969 and 1987), for patients who learn they have a terminal disease, e.g., cancer or AIDS. These stages are:

1. **Shock** — Individual is informed that he or she is being terminated as of a certain date.

2. **Denial** — This really is not going to happen to me, there has been a mistake in putting my name on the list.

3. **Anger** — It is not fair, Joe Doaks is not on the list and I have done a better job than he. My boss was unfair in my last performance appraisal. They are terminating me after 30 years of faithful service because of my age, etc.

4. **Depression** — I have let my family down, we will have to sell our home and move, the children will have to change schools, I am a failure, etc.

5. **Bargaining** — Maybe if I go to my boss and apologize for the negative remark I made he or she will reconsider, perhaps they would keep me on if I offered to take a salary cut, maybe we will get that new defense contract and then they can keep me, etc.

6. **Acceptance** — I guess there is no possibility of keeping my job so I had better get busy and find a new job. I think my career counselor can really help me so I am going to cooperate fully and follow up on all of his or her suggestions.

It is important that the professional career counselor assist the outplaced employee in working through the first five stages as quickly as possible, although in some cases it may take months to do so. Until stage 6 (acceptance) is reached, the outplaced person may have great difficulty in properly functioning in a job interview. This person must not only have all of the tools to successfully compete in the job market, but should also have a positive mental attitude and high level of enthusiasm to be a viable candidate.

Ideally, the professional career counselor has been consulted by an outplacing company prior to cuts being announced. The career counselor then can suggest the best time and way to make the announcement, and agree on the services which he or she will perform. The career counselor should meet with outplaced employee(s) as soon as the company has made the announcement. I worked with one company where I sat in an adjoining conference room when employees were advised they were being terminated. Each terminated employee was notified individually by the company management. They were then introduced to me, and I explained what services I offered. In several cases I took the terminated employee to lunch which gave us a much better opportunity to get acquainted. At this luncheon and subsequent meetings in my office we discussed how the news of the termination should be communicated to his or her family. We then laid out an action plan and schedule aimed at getting the employee successfully placed.

Frequently a terminated long-term employee is devastated by the news. Depression can set in fairly quickly (Stage 4). One outplaced client became suicidal and talked of divorcing his wife (prior to this he had a good marriage) because he was a "loser" and she would be better off without him. These problems had to be immediately addressed prior to getting on with the job search process. Where possible the spouse should also receive counseling. Whether or not the spouse is working, job loss is very threatening and will result in a substantial change in the family's standard of living if the outplaced employee does not obtain a comparable job prior to expiration of the company's benefits.

Assessment Instruments — The career counselor in private practice must decide if and what type of a assessment instruments will be used, and for what types of clients and career counseling. Diane Shepard covers this subject in depth in Chapter Five.

Career Library — The counselor needs to plan the resources and types of material to be included in the career library. The career library should include Department of Labor publications, career magazines, employer directories, work books, college catalogs, state and professional publications, audio tapes and possibly video tapes. The appendix lists the contents of the career resource library used in my practice. It should be noted that this library has continued to grow during the past eight years of my private practice. Homework is assigned to clients between sessions and the career resource library is a source of material for this purpose. In addition I have clipped many articles relating to career planning and development from newspapers, and magazines, and this material is also used to help clients.

It is also recommended that you become familiar with the material in your public library and assign such material as *Standard and Poor's Register* as homework or source material for researching potential employers. I urge my outplacement clients to review the want ads in the Sunday paper and spend Sunday afternoon in the library researching the companies of interest. Information obtained on the companies can then be included in cover letters. These cover letters can be drafted Sunday evening or early Monday so they can be typed on Monday and mailed prior to the last mail pick-up on that day.

Private Practice Incorporation — For a new practice a decision must be made as to whether to incorporate or to "do business as." States have different rules and regulations for incorporating. To determine the procedure in your state contact your state's Secretary of State. If you incorporate send a copy of your By-Laws and Constitution (if you have one) to the IRS and obtain a company identification number which you will use for tax returns. If you do not incorporate you will need to declare your business expenses and revenue on the proper schedule of your personal federal and state tax returns.

Advantages of incorporation include protecting your practice's name (register it with your state) and some shielding of your personal assets. If your practice fails and you are forced to seek bankruptcy protection the creditors could not claim your personal assets (home, cars, etc.). In the event of a liability suit, incorporation may also provide some protection of your personal assets. Another advantage of incorporation is the option of having a board of directors that represents different areas of expertise. My practice, Career Counselor Services, Inc. has a board of seven members. Current board membership includes an accountant, a project manager, the owner of an employment agency, two homemakers, a teacher, and a partner in an engineering firm. These board members provide many helpful suggestions and are also a source of client referrals.

Disadvantages of incorporation are the expense and effort of obtaining incorporation, the need to file different types of tax forms with the IRS and your state, and complying with your state's rules and regulations governing corporations.

A counselor planning to enter private practice should consult with an attorney and an accountant that specialize in business organization to determine what is involved in your state relative to incorporation. Whether or not you incorporate you need to decide how much salary you are going to pay yourself and then file the appropriate Federal FICA form quarterly. You also must file estimated Federal and state income tax forms quarterly along with the tax payment.

Marketing Plan — Mike Shahnasarian, in Chapter Six, describes in detail how he developed his marketing plan. Note that it is important to measure results (client sources) against marketing effort (sales and advertising), and adjust the plan accordingly. To be successful a private practice must have a sufficient number of satisfied, paying clients (customers).

Unfortunately, career counselors do not have the same public recognition as other private practice professionals, e.g., physicians, dentists, attorneys and psychologists, all of whom are licensed by the state which sets minimum standards. In addition, the state prohibits people from performing these services unless they are licensed by the state. Currently about 30 states license or certify counselors, but none specifically license or certify career counselors. No state prohibits anyone, regardless of background, from calling themselves career counselors or from attempting to provide many of the services provided by National Certified Career Counselors. I frequently receive telephone inquiries asking what do I do and what are my charges? These calls rarely result in a client as there are a number of "career counseling" firms in the yellow pages that quote lower rates and spend more money on advertising. I have, on some occasions, told the caller that I am surprised they have not asked me about my qualifications to conduct career counseling. This seems to be a surprising thought to the caller. When a person looks under physician, dentist or attorney in the yellow pages it is automatically assumed those listed are qualified in their specialty area. This is a misplaced trust when it comes to career counseling — even more so than for family or personal counseling.

It is also obvious that many people are unclear about the role of career counselor. Even though I am listed in the yellow pages under "Career and Vocational Counseling" the frequent question is "Are you an employment agency?" The public education system teaches children in health or hygiene classes that they should go to a dentist twice a year to have their teeth checked and should also obtain a physical examination periodically from a physician, but in school do children learn that if they are having difficulty in finding a satisfying vocation they should consult a qualified career counselor? In many school systems the guidance counselors are so busy with class scheduling, student discipline problems, writing letters of recommendation to colleges, administering standardized achievement tests, or personal counseling that little or no career counseling is conducted. Should we then be surprised that so many college students are unsure of their college major, or change college major one or more times (Gordon, 1984; Haislett & Hafer, 1990)? Should we be surprised that so many new liberal arts college graduates have difficulty finding an occupation that requires a college degree and is compatible with their occupational interests?

What are the implications of all this to the career counselor? It might be presumed that the lack of good career planning advice at the secondary and postsecondary levels would result in a flood of potential clients to career counselors. This is not so. Most people are so naive when it comes to career development that they have difficulty in identifying resources which could assist them. Many go to an employment agency or the state job service and expect that a job consistent with their abilities, interests and values will be forthcoming. When this does not occur they then become frustrated, depressed and disillusioned. Others have heard horror stories about people who have gone to so-called "career counselors", have been charged a large sum up front, and received very little helpful service.

Another category of persons who need career counseling are the unemployed. Since their only income may be on unemployment payment they are understandably reluctant to take on an additional financial obligation. The counselor in private practice needs to recognize the above dynamics and factor them into his or her marketing plan.

Financial Plan — Both Mike Shahnasarian in Chapter Six and Frank Karpati in Chapter Seven discuss material and considerations needed for the office's financial plan. An annual financial plan is important for both those already in private practice and those planning to enter the field. If you plan to borrow money to start a private practice you will need a well thought out financial plan to present to the financing agency. Help in developing your financial plan and learning how to obtain a loan is often available from your local branch of SCORE, Service Corps of Retired Executives, sponsored by the U.S. Small Business Administration. There is no charge for this service.

Other Business and Counseling Considerations — The successful career counselor in private practice is an entrepreneur and must approach the private practice from a business viewpoint. If you are not sure you fit this mold read the book *Working for yourself: Career planning information* (1988). It is not enough to be an expert in career counseling or to have a burning desire to have your own business. The majority of new businesses fail within the first five years.

Careful plans must therefore be made prior to launching the private practice to give it the best chance of success. Areas that must be considered include:

1. Counseling approach — Ed Herr discusses this subject in Chapter Two. Mary-Lynne Musgrove (Chapter Four) and Diane Shepard (Chapter Five) also provide valuable input relative to counseling approach in private practice.

2. Types of clients — Chapter Two also covers this subject.

3. Certification and licensure — Are you a National Certified Career Counselor? Does your state license counselors, and if so are you licensed? It is strongly recommended that a career counselor in private practice be both certified and licensed in order to project the proper professional image.

4. Competition — A survey of the potential competition should be made. Determine types of clients, services offered, fees, resources, office locations, and qualifications of counselors. The yellow pages of the phone book are a good starting point. Also check to see if local colleges provide career counseling to non-students or alumni. Mike Shahnasarian in Chapter Six discusses this subject in detail.

5. Private practice entry mode — The least risky way of entering private practice is to have another job and begin a private practice part-time. Some clients prefer to meet in the evenings or weekends anyway, as they are considering a career change while retaining a full-time day job. Maintaining another job and conducting the private practice part-time obviates the need for the counselor to initially draw a salary from the private practice.

Client Payment Schedule — The self-employed counselor must first develop a policy regarding payment for counseling services. Is the counselor going to require payment at the end of each session or after a block of sessions? Normally I require payment at the end of each session, but occasionally will agree to a later, specific payment schedule. In the case of corporate clients, e.g., outplacement counseling, I bill the company monthly for services provided in the previous month. This can present a cash flow problem which must be recognized and factored into the office's financial planning.

Business Records — Whether the career counselor decides to incorporate or not he or she needs to determine how the practice's financial records are to be maintained, and set up a bookkeeping system that will serve the needs of the business. I would recommend obtaining an IBM compatible microcomputer with a minimum of 640K RAM and 30 MB hard disk. Software is also important. CCS uses "First Choice" (word processor, data base manager, report generator, mailing labels, etc.), "DAC EASY Accounting" (financial records) and "First Publisher" (desk top publisher). The computerized accounting system has made it possible for CCS to maintain all of the financial records and prepare tax returns without retaining the services of an accountant. If a counselor is not familiar with microcomputers, computer courses are available at local community colleges.

Record System — In addition to financial records, the office must have a record system for clients and the overall business. Norma Zuber covers client records in Chapter Three and Frank Karpati both business and clients records in Chapter Seven.

Ethics

In view of recent scandals in the financial community, federal government, business, state governments and other institutions, it appears appropriate to address the subject of ethics. We should also recognize that many in the general public also view "career counseling services" with some suspicion as a result of unqualified practitioners and irresponsible advertising.

If the career counselor is a member of the American Association for Counseling and Development (AACD), the National Career Development Association (NCDA), is a National Certified Counselor (NCC), a National Certified Career Counselor (NCCC), and a Licensed Professional Counselor (PC), then the counselor is bound by four different ethical codes. The AACD, NCDA and National Board for Certified Counselors (NBCC) have each issued their own ethical code. In addition, states granting licensure or certification, have their own rules, regulations and ethical codes. Since I am a member of the AACD and NCDA, an NCC, an NCCC and an LPC, I must comply with all of these ethical codes. It is important that the practicing counselor be familiar with all applicable codes as non-compliance could result in censure, loss of certification and license, and possible legal action, in the case of state licensure laws. In addition, violation of these ethics codes could result in civil liability suits. Usually good judgement should prevent the career counselor from having these problems, but lack of understanding of the codes could cause a career counselor to be vulnerable.

NCDA has issued a document entitled, *Section C: Consumer Guidelines For Selecting a Career Counselor* (1988). I normally provide my clients with these guidelines at our initial session. Quoted below are several extracts from this document which should be considered relative to making promises to clients, or in advertising your services.

> "Ask any counselor you are considering for a detailed explanation of services (career counseling, testing, employment search strategy planning, resume writing, etc.). Make sure you understand the service, your degree of involvement, and your financial commitment.

> "Fees — Select a counselor who is professionally trained, who specifies fees and services upon request, and who lets you choose the services you desire. Make certain you can terminate the services at any time, paying only for services rendered.

> "Promises — Be skeptical of services that make promises of more money, better jobs, resumes that get speedy results, or an immediate solution to career problems.

> "Ethical Practices — Professional career counselors are expected to follow the ethical guidelines of organizations such as the National Career Development Association, the National Board for Certified Counselors, the American Association for Counseling and Development, or the American Psychological Association. Professional codes of ethics advise against grandiose guarantees and promises, exorbitant fees, and breaches of confidentiality, among other things. You may wish to ask for a detailed explanation of services offered, your financial and time commitments, and a copy of the ethical guidelines used by the career counselor or service you are considering."

The National Board for Certified Counselors has issued a document entitled *Counseling Services: Consumer Rights and Responsibilities* which is also appropriate to give to clients. Frank Karpati, in Chapter Seven, discusses this in more detail and the document is shown in Figure 7-8.

The following paragraphs sum up a majority of the requirements contained in the four ethical codes. At the end of each item the applicable code(s) are shown, in brackets, by the following designations: AACD, NECC, NCDA, SCLPC, and All (means all of the preceding four codes).

I have also indicated for LPC the ethical code of the State of South Carolina for licensed professional counselors, as an example of a state ethical code. If you are licensed in another state you should check your state requirements. Please keep in mind my comments on the various code requirements are not a legal opinion. If in doubt on a particular point you may desire to consult an attorney. In addition, if any of these points should be involved in litigation, the court proceedings would be the final authority.

Advertising of Counseling Services — The counselor must accurately inform the public of professional services, expertise, and techniques of counseling available. Information must not contain false, inaccurate, misleading, partial, out-of-context, or deceptive material or statements (All).

Assessment Instruments (A.I.s.) — Counselor must use A.I.s. approach for the client, understand the norms, and properly administer and interpret the results (AACD, NBCC, NCDA). See Chapter Five for additional information on this subject.

Boundaries of Counselor's Competence — Provide only those services and use only those techniques for which the counselor is qualified by training or experience (All).

Client in Another Counseling Relationship — If potential client is already in a counseling relationship with another professional, the counselor should not accept the client without first contacting and receiving the approval of that other professional. If the counselor discovers later that this situation exists the counselor must gain the consent of the other professional or terminate the relationship, unless the client elects to terminate the other relationship (All).

Computerized Assessment — The counselor must adequately explain the limitations of computer technology and observe precautions previously stated for assessment instruments (AACD, NBCC, NCDA). See Chapter Five for additional information on this subject.

Confidentiality of Client Records — Client information must be kept confidential except as agreed to by the client in writing, except under certain prescribed situations. Records are to be safeguarded accordingly (All). Note, under South Carolina law LPC/Client information is "privileged" and cannot be subpoenaed. A court order is required to obtain this information.

Consultation with Another Professional — The counselor may choose to consult about the client problem with another competent professional. NBCC also states that the counselor must notify the client of this right. Under South Carolina law the licensed professional counselor would need the client's written permission for this consultation (All).

Counseling Goals — The counselor must inform the client of the goals, purposes, techniques, rules of procedure, and limitations of the counseling process. (All).

Cultural Differences — Counselors must guard the rights and personal dignity of the client through an awareness of biases based on ethnicity, race, etc. Culturally relevant techniques should be used. Caution should be used in evaluating and interpreting A.I. performances of minority clients (All).

Danger of Clients to Themselves and Others — If the client indicates there is clear and imminent danger to the client (potential suicide) or to others, the counselor must take reasonable action or inform responsible authorities. Consultation with other professionals must be used where possible (All). Examples of possible action would be to advise the state department of social services in cases of incest, referral to a psychotherapist, psychologist, or psychiatrist, advising a spouse of potential murder, etc. Career counselors are less likely to encounter some of these problems than psychotherapists, but action must be taken in all appropriate cases.

Dual Relationships — When the counselor has other relationships, particularly of an administrative, supervisory, and/or evaluative nature with a person seeking career counseling, the counselor should refer the individual to another professional. Dual relationships with clients that might impair the counselor's objectivity and professional judgment (e.g., as with close friends or relatives), must be avoided and referred to another professional (All). The South Carolina Ethical Code specifies that the counselor shall avoid dual relationships with students, employees, and supervisees that could impair their professional judgement or increase the risk of exploitation. Another undesirable situation would be for a professor to counsel one of his or her students or student's family members. As an adjunct faculty member teaching a graduate course in career counseling, one of my students expressed a desire to send her adolescent child to me for career counseling. I had to tell her this would represent a conflict of interest and made a referral.

Gather Data on Effectiveness of Counseling — The career counselor should follow up on clients to determine if the counseling achieved the agreed to purposes and goals. Based upon the findings, the counselor should modify the counseling process as appropriate (AACD, NBCC, NCDA).

Ethical Behavior of Other Professional Colleagues or Associates — When information relative to other counselors is possessed that raises doubt as to the ethical behavior of another counselor, action must be taken to attempt to rectify the condition, whether the counselor is or is not an AACD, NCDA member or an NCCC. Action should use institution channels first if the offending counselor is employed by an institution. Then if the situation is not remedied, or the counselor does not work for an institution, even part time, the situation should be reported to the AACD Ethics Committee and NBCC (All). In the case of South Carolina the counselor should bring the unethical conduct to the attention of the State Board of Examiners for the Licensure of Professional Counselors, Associate Counselors, and Marital and Family Therapists.

Finding Comparable Services — If the career counselor's fee structure is inappropiate for a client, assistance must be provided to help the client find comparable services of acceptable cost (All).

Institutional Affiliation — It is unethical to use an institutional affiliation to recruit clients for one's private practice. A college counselor educator or counseling center counselor should not counsel students from the college in a private practice (All).

Minors — Counselors working with minors or persons who are unable to give consent to the counseling goals, purposes, techniques, etc. must protect the client's best interests (AACD). I obtain agreement at the beginning of counseling with adolescents and their parents as to who will receive my final written report covering the results of the counseling process.

Professional Growth — Counselors are expected to improve professional practices, teaching, services and research for career counseling. Professional growth should be continuous and recognize the need for continuing education to ensure competent service (All).

Public Behavior that Violates Moral and Legal Standards — Career counselors must avoid public behavior that is clearly in violation of accepted moral and legal standards (NBCC, NCDA). It is suggested that if the counselor has questions relative to the appropriateness of specific behavior he/she should consult with the AACD and NCDA Ethics Committees, NBCC and/or state licensure board.

Referrals — If the counselor feels unable to be of professional assistance to the client, the counselor must either avoid initiating the counseling relationship or immediately terminate counseling. In either event the counselor must suggest appropriate alternatives (All.)

Sexual Harassment — Counselors do not condone or engage in sexual harassment, which is defined as deliberate or repeated comments, gestures, or physical contacts of a sexual nature (All). The Code of

Ethics of South Carolina specifically prohibits sexual harassment of clients, students, employees, trainees, supervisees, or colleagues (SCLPC). It should be noted that there are also federal laws which prohibit sexual harassment.

Sexual Intimacy — Counselors shall avoid any type of sexual intimacies or sexual relationships with clients (AACD, SCLPC). It should be noted that this is the basis for many liability suites against psychologists and counselors. A good practice is to see clients only in your office at scheduled appointments. The South Carolina LPC Ethics Code prohibits sexual activities with clients both during counseling and for six months thereafter.

Terminating Counseling Relationships — The counseling relationship should be terminated whenever the counselor and/or the client feels that no further benefits are likely to accrue to the client, or the counselor does not have the necessary expertise to assist the client further. Termination should also occur if the relationship violates the ethical codes, or the mental or physical condition of the counselor makes it difficult to carry out an effective professional relationship. As discussed under "Referral" it may be appropriate for the counselor to make a referral at this point (All).

Supplementary Information

During the NCDA workshop discussed in the Preface, attendees asked questions at the end of each presentation. As the seven panel members responded to questions, it became obvious that in many cases there is no single "right" answer. For example, use of assessment instruments in career counseling varied considerably from no use by one counselor to frequent use by other counselors. It was clear that there were many different ways of conducting a successful career counseling private practice.

At the end of most chapters is an addendum containing additional information provided by the panel during the question and answer portion of the workshop. Some of the material provided in the addenda by the editor is supplementary information not covered in the workshop due to time limitations.

Bradley, L.J. (1990) *Counseling midlife career changers.* Garrett Park, MD: Garrett Park Press.

Brown, S.T., & Brown, D. (1990). *Designing and implementing a career information center.* Garrett Park, MD: Garrett Park Press.

Brown, D., & Minor, C.W. (Eds.) (1989). *Working in America: A status report on planning and problems.* Alexandria, VA: National Career Development Association.

Code of ethics. (1987). Alexandria, VA: National Board for Certified Counselors.

Ethical standards. (1988). Alexandria, VA: American Association for Counseling and Development.

Gordon, V.N. (1984). *The undecided college student.* Springfield, IL: Charles C. Thomas.

Haislett, J., & Hafer, A.A. (1990). Predicting success of engineering students during the freshman year. *The Career Development Quarterly, 39*(1), 86-95.

Kapes, J.T., & Mastie, M.M. (Eds.). (1988). *A counselor's guide to career assessment instruments.* 2nd Edition. Alexandria, VA: National Career Development Association.

Kubler-Ross, E. (1969). *On death and dying.* New York: Macmillan Publishing Co., Inc.

Kubler-Ross. E. (1987). *AIDS: The ultimate challenge.* New York: Macmillan Publishing Co.

Leibowitz, Z., & Lea, D. (Eds.) (1986). *Adult career development.* Alexandria, VA: National Career Development Association.

Montross, D.H., & Shinkman, C.J. (Eds.) (1981). *Career development in the 1980s: Theory and practice.* Springfield, IL: Charles C. Thomas.

Section C: Consumer guidelines for selecting a career counselor. (1988). In *The professional practice of career counseling and consultation: A resource document.* Alexandria, VA: The National Career Development Association.

Section E: National Career Development Association Ethical Standards. (1988) In *The professional practice of career counseling and consultation: A resource document.* Alexandria, VA: The National Career Development Association.

Seminar proves value of AACD insurance plan. (May 30, 1991) *Guidepost, 33*(17), 21.

South Carolina code of ethics. (1987). Columbia, SC: Board of Examiners for Licensure of Professional Counselors, Associate Counselors, and Marital and Family Therapists.

Working for yourself: Career planning information. (1988). Eugene, OR: National Career Information System.

Chapter Two — Types of Career Counseling Practices

Edwin L. Herr
Division of Counseling and
Educational Psychology and
Career Studies
Pennsylvania State University

As one enters a career counseling practice and stays in it, two matters are of special concern: (1) what type of services will you provide or what kinds of career counseling will you offer; and (2) with what types of client will you work? Obviously, one must answer these questions when preparing initial publicity about the practice. For example, one can decide to offer individual counseling, group counseling, or both. One can require testing of all clients or tailor testing to the specific needs of certain clients. One can provide assessment of clients on a referral basis for other counselors or psychologists, for such agencies as the Office of Vocational Rehabilitation, or for employers. If so, one must be willing to provide written reports of client interviews and test results in a professional manner and have available forms by which clients can permit release of such information to specific recipients. One can provide workshops for groups of clients on job search techniques, career planning, college choices, anger management and other areas of one's expertise. One can include as a part of one's practice consultation about human resource development or career services with business, industry or government. One may propose an employment assistance program for employees of a corporation.

Along with deciding what services to provide, it helps to determine the prime client groups one hopes to serve: adolescents, adults, persons having work adjustment problems, recovering alcoholics, women returning to the work place, older workers contemplating retirement, persons in the midst of career change, dislocated workers, retirees, or all of these. Such decisions will guide the types of tests and resource material you need to have available in your practice. If you have a computer, the type of clients you serve will shape the software you use. Decisions about the populations to be served will affect how you publicize your practice and to whom you send your publicity.

Types of Career Counseling Practice

But, implicit in the services you offer and the clients you hope to serve is the definition or type of career counseling you embrace. Do you, for example, adopt the view of Zunker (1986) that career counseling tends to embrace components or strategies that differ for diverse populations. For example, according to Zunker, career counseling for adults in career transition would include seven components or strategies: experience identification, interest identification, skills identification, value and needs identification, education/training planning, occupational planning, and concludes with the development of a life learning plan (pp. 236-248). In this view, career counseling for women would include such components or strategies as job-search skills, working climate, life-style skills, and support and follow-up (pp. 262-265). Within his conception of career counseling, Zunker uses broad terminology that others might define as more guidance than counseling but this perspective is very useful in its emphasis on wedding the special characteristics of different populations to the treatments or strategies they receive.

Or, do you conceptualize career counseling as teaching as does Healy (1982). According to Healy, "The implications of conceptualizing counseling as teaching are that a counselor helps a person who is having difficulty coping with everyday concerns by creating an atmosphere conducive to learning and by guiding the person through a sequence of exercises that provide information, teach skills, or develop habits" (pp. 166-167). In this view, career counseling is specialized counseling focused on career implementations and planning. The career counselor helps a client to generate and to use personal and career information, to obtain and to interpret experiences relevant to careers, to set goals and to solve problems, and to evaluate progress" (pp. 173). In addition, in this view, "Counselors prescribe individual learning strategies and join clients in making the strategies work. The process of individualizing has four stages: (1) establishing client needs, goals, and obstacles to them; (2) identifying and then selecting particular strategies; (3) teaching and assisting the client in implementing solutions; and (4) verifying accomplishment of the solution and achievement of the goal" (p. 175).

You may think of career counseling as does Isaacson (1985) who suggests that, "Career counseling, like counseling in general, requires the counselor to identify properly and respond appropriately to feelings, thoughts, attitudes, and behaviors expressed by the client and to assist the client to developing desired and appropriate behaviors that reflect the increasing understanding and insight resulting from counseling. Further, it requires the counselor to be competent in assisting the client in acquiring, processing, and applying information and skills required in effective decision making and subsequent implementation of plans" (p. 98).

Further, you may take an even more psychological view of career counseling as do Crites (1981) or Brown (1985). Crites (1981) has suggested that as insights from client-centered and psychodynamic approaches have been applied to career counseling, choice problems are viewed as essentially personality problems. Therefore, the assumptions that guide the provision of career counseling need to be considered in relation to personal adjustment counseling or psychotherapy. Crites uses the term career counseling to refer

specifically to an interpersonal process focused upon assisting an individual to make an appropriate career decision. "Ideally, it involves active participation in the decisional process, not simply passive-receptive input of information" (p. 11). For Crites, career counseling is both more and less than personal adjustment counseling or psychotherapy. "Vocational and personal problems are different, but they do interact. Thus, career counseling often embraces personal counseling but it goes beyond this to explore and replicate the client's role in the main area of life — the world of work" (p. 11).

Brown (1985) pushes the interaction of career counseling and personal counseling even further than does Crites. Brown, who defines career counseling "as the process of helping an individual select, prepare for, enter, and function effectively in an occupation" (p. 197), views career counseling "as a viable intervention with clients that have rather severe emotional problems." In particular, Brown distinguishes between clients who have intrapsychic (cognitive or emotional) problems and those persons who work in a non-supportive, stress-producing environment that may cause symptoms that appear to be intrapsychic, mental health disorders rather than functions of poor personal work environment fit.

These are not the only ways one can conceive of career counseling in private practice. Nor are they mutually exclusive. But, I am personally convinced that how you align yourself with these points of emphasis will largely determine what you do in your private practice and how you convey yourself to your potential client groups. For example, I am personally committed to the notion that unless I am willing to look at the interaction of career counseling and behavior health or mental health problems, there is little likelihood that I can be effective in assisting persons with job adjustment problems, dislocated workers, spouses of those experiencing job dislocations, or recovering alcoholics. Obviously, you may choose not to work with such populations or to work only with populations whose needs for information or decision-making skills are more straightforward.

The point I am concerned about here is that how one thinks about oneself as a career counselor in private practice, how one defines the skills and processes to be embodied in career counseling, and how one publicizes these perspectives will limit or open more broadly the populations you serve. Obviously how distinctions are made by the career counselor about the type of career counseling practice to be implemented will determine whether the therapeutic approach focuses upon intrapsychic changes, as in personal counseling and psychotherapy, or on altering the work environment or choosing another work environment through career counseling, or on assisting the individual to manage the stress induced in such an environment, or on dealing specifically with career exploration and planning about a specific job, an occupation, a major in college, or a training opportunity. The view one takes of these matters can constrain or enlarge the range of problems likely to be addressed by career counseling and the populations you are likely to serve.

Personally, I believe in an eclectic view of career counseling and in differential treatment (Herr & Cramer, 1988). As a result, I see a wide range of populations for a large spectrum of career related problems. I believe such a view is consistent with the 1985 *Consumer Guidelines for Selecting a Career Counselor* adopted by the National Career Development Association. Under the heading, "What do Career Counselors do?" the following is stated:

> The services of career counselors differ, depending on competence. A professional or National Certified Career Counselor helps people make decisions and plans related to life/career directions. The strategies and techniques are tailored to the specific needs of the person seeking help. It is likely that the career counselor will do one or more of the following:
> - conduct individual and group personal counseling sessions to help clarify life/career goals.
> - administer and interpret tests and inventories to assess abilities, interests, etc., and to identify career options.
> - encourage exploratory activities through assignments and planning experiences.
> - utilize career planning systems and occupational information systems to help individuals better understand the world of work.
> - provide opportunities for improving decision-making skills.
> - assist in developing individualized career plans.
> - teach job-hunting strategies and skills and assist in the development of resumes.

- help resolve potential personal conflicts on the job through practice in human relations skills.
- assist in understanding the integration of work and other life roles.
- provide support for persons experiencing job stress, job loss, career transition (pp. 1-2).

Within these guidelines, it is apparent that the type of career counseling practice one engages in should be based on one's competence, training and experience, and on one's constant implementation of ethical standards.

My Own Career Counseling Practice

Let me turn briefly to my own private practice to further consider the types of career counseling and the types of clients with which I am involved. I am in practice with two colleagues, a male and a female, in an organization called Career Counseling, Consultation, and Assessment Associates (C^3A^2). Two of us have doctoral degrees; one, a master's plus. All three of us are National Certified Counselors and National Certified Career Counselors and two of us are also licensed psychologists in Pennsylvania. We each describe ourselves as career counselors although on our brochure we indicate that our full credentials include that we are licensed psychologists. Our primary clientele are persons concerned about job changes, initial job choice, or career planning in general and tend to include high school and college students as well as adults of all ages. Perhaps because our brochure indicates that two of us are career counselors and licensed psychologists, I find that we have a large number of persons who use the career rubric to come to see me or my associates for a lot of reasons which may start with a career problem but that such a problem is clearly interactive with other aspects of their life that must be considered and dealt with if the career problem is to be resolved.

To help you anticipate the types of career counseling problems you may be expected to deal with in your practice as a way of helping you decide which of these cases you would deal with and those you would refer, I have disguised and slightly modified vignettes of recent presenting problems of clients with whom I have worked. They include:
- A recovering alcoholic couple trying to reestablish a place in the work force, or begin an entrepreneurial enterprise (a domestic cleaning business), or at age 40 leave the family business which has been an oppressive and domineering situation for years;
- A recovering alcoholic who also has a bi-polar disorder (manic-depressive), is single in the 30's, with compulsive sexual behavior (100's of sex partners), concerned about AIDS,

27

bright but never committed to a career. Denies responsibility for his jagged career pattern, in part because he is afraid of how his father and two older brothers will react to his choice because they are all successful physicians.

- A woman, aged 40, with several failed marriages, unhappy at work because she is underemployed. She is bright and multiply talented but has reentered the work force late and is in a job beneath her performance abilities and her capabilities to manage or supervise others. She is now being supervised by a younger woman whose competence she does not respect and who she threatens. She has also experienced bouts of depression and suicide ideation associated with a long-standing conflict with her father who is a high achiever and has been very demanding of her throughout life. She feels she does not come up to his standards.
- A liberal arts graduate who has no idea what she wants to do about a job or about graduate school.
- Several high school students attempting to choose a college and a major. In some cases, they simply need information and reasurance or a strategy by which to proceed. In another case, the student's father is totally negative about the boy's motivation or abilities and does not want to pay for him to go to college even though he is quite able to do so and the mother has a good job as well. We are trying to look at the consequences of different educational opportunities or the military or work and part-time school, the possible effect of the boy's learning disabilities, and indeed, the father's attitudes toward the boy.
- A social worker in a rehabilitation agency who is burned out and is, indeed, far more oriented by tests and abilities to retailing and interior design than human services.
- A minister and his wife who are poverty stricken after 23 years of ministry; who decided to leave the ministry, after some unfortunate and negative behavior among their congregation. They have no retirement benefits because they served in independent, fundamentalist congregations. They have no idea what jobs or further training could be open to them; no idea of the elasticity of the skills developed in the ministry. Wife trained as a nurse but has not been involved in patient care for years and has no confidence that she can return to that role. Husband has stress-related hives and other complications as a result of the career crisis they are in.
- A foreman who needs help with anger management because of a temper about to get him fired; really does not have a behavioral repertoire by which to discriminate different types of anger situations and the appropriate response.

- A minister who is highly stressed because his church building burned down. He is bearing a tremendous emotional burden in helping the congregation cope with the grief and mourning of this loss.
- A university assistant professor who was denied the opportunity for tenure because his department head is threatened by him, not because of lack of productivity. Needs to examine organizational norms and how he can avoid such problems in the future if he stays in academe.
- A 40 year old man whose severe allergies keep him from pursuing a lot of career options in which he is interested in biology and the outdoors; recently got married late to a woman who had a child and from whom he is now separated; and who continues to try to live out his mother's aspirations for him to be perfect, unlike his father.
- A waiter with a B.A. and a master's degree from a Christian college which has not given him much credibility in the job market and he is concerned about next steps.
- A registered nurse who wants to reenter the work force but not in the area of her training because she feels incompetent and out of touch. Trying to determine if there is any elasticity in her background — now studying to be a medical records technician.
- Several college students whose major motivation has been partying. Now experiencing separation anxiety and the emotional impact of not acquiring the career skills that many employers want them to have. Concerned about next steps and how they can recover some credibility in the work place.
- An adopted Asian child who has some learning difficulties, but is social and athletic. Parents want her to go to a vocational school or to the military.
- An art student who had to leave school for failing grades but who was experiencing allergies and TMJ problems that reduced his energies and ability to be task oriented for long periods. Has lost some motivation to return to school but is interested in reviewing his options now that his physical problems are under control.
- A fifty year old former service technician who has experienced a disabling leg injury and who now needs to consider retraining possibilities and different types of sedentary work for which he might qualify. As a high school graduate measures on tests of mental ability as capably as a college graduate.

These are enough vignettes to allow you to sense the range of problems and counselor skills required in a private practice like the one in which I am a partner. To add to this inventory of the types of problems I typically experience as a counselor, my associates and I have recently become a sub-contractor with a Private Industry Council to assist them in doing outplacement counseling for firms involved in downsizing. At the time I write this, we are working with four waves of workers who have been terminated from a defense contractor which does high technlogy research and development. We are offering individual counseling and workshops on job search, stress management, and other techniques to these workers. In addition, I am doing workshops and group counseling with the terminated workers and their spouses, a challenging but, I think, important service.

As I am sure is obvious to you, I see career counseling as broader and more personal, indeed in many cases as a mental health modality, than do many other theorists or practitioners. I do not contend that you should see career counseling as I do or that you should engage in the types of career counseling practices that my colleagues and I do. However, I think that it is important that you do not drift into private practice without considering very carefully your competencies, your training and experience, your professional commitment to a view or views of career counseling which can guide your definition of the services you will offer and the types of clients you will serve. The assessments and resources you will need as well as the image you will want to convey in your publicity about your practice depend upon such professional definition.

Additional Thoughts on
"Types of Career Counseling Practices"

Herr — If a third party is provided with any information on the client, a release form must be obtained from the client specifically delineating what information may be released and to whom. The career counselor should develop, with the client, a plan of action resulting from the counseling. A plan relative to anger management

is appropriate for some clients. In outplacement counseling it may be desirable to have a session with the husband and wife together. Generally it is desirable to give the client appropriate homework.

Shahnasarian — Clients are generally in the mid 20s to early 40s age range. Corporate and outplacement is about 50% of the career counseling and retail (individual) career counseling clients the other 50%.

Shepard — Clients are in the 30s, 40s and 50s age range and 90% are males. Most clients are self referrals or corporate training.

Karpati — 80% of clients relate to college career counseling.

Hafer — About 80% of clients are male and 20% are female. Client distribution by reason for career counseling has been as follows:

Career change	— 30%
Lack of full time employment	— 30
Occupational/Employee dissatisfaction	— 20
Occupational/College Major/College selection	— 11
Outplacement	— 5

Client age range distribution has been as follows:

Adolescents	7%
20s Age Range	5
30s Age Range	32
40s Age Range	28
50s Age Range	28

Brown, D. (1985) Career counseling: Before, after, or instead of personal counseling? *The Vocational Guidance Quarterly. 33*(3), 197-201.

Crites, J. O. (1981). *Career counseling: Models, methods, and materials.* New York: McGraw-Hill.

Healy, C. C. (1982) *Career development. Counseling through the life stages.* Boston: Allyn & Bacon, Inc.

Herr, E. L., & Cramer, S.H. (1988). *Career guidance and counseling through the life span: Systematic approaches.* Glenview, Illinois: Scott Foresman and Company.

Isaacson, L. E. (1985). *Basics of career counseling.* Boston: Allyn & Bacon, Inc.

National Career Development Association. (1985). Consumer guidelines for selecting a career counselor. *Career Development, 1*(2), 1-2.

National Commission on Jobs and Small Business (1986). *10,000,000 jobs* Washington; National Commission on Jobs and Small Business.

Nollen, S. D. (1982). *New work schedules in practice.* New York; Van Nostrand.

Sinetar, M. (1989). *Do what you love, the money will follow: Discovering your right livelihood.* New York: Dell.

Strasser, S. (1990). *Transitions: Successful strategies from mid-career to retirement.* Hawthorne, NJ: Career Press.

Zunker, V. (1986). *Career counseling: Applied concepts of life planning.* Monterey, CA: Brooks/Cole.

Chapter Three — Career Development Counseling: Intake and Information

Norma Zuber
Career and Life Planning
Norma Zuber & Associates
Ventura, CA

In the very exciting process of career counseling, the intake and information process is the first and an important step. Although this initial contact is usually called the "intake interview," in most cases the event far exceeds the simple gathering of background data. It is the time for the counselor to begin to observe the client, to establish rapport, to assess the client's needs and to sense any obstacles or stumbling blocks that may need to be alleviated before successful career planning can take place. Counseling goals must be established and clarified and a plan of action developed. The counselor needs to set in place some basic flexible methods for achieving fundamental goals, for obtaining relevant information from the client and for providing information to the client on the career counseling process and the counselor's credentials and abilities (Yost & Corbishley, 1987). It is important to explain the process, to establish ground rules and to present the practitioner's qualifications and the specific services offered.

Some standardized methods for recording information should be implemented from the outset. A practical method to obtain and record pertinent information in a logical progression is through the use of an intake form such as the "Student Career Development Record" developed at Westmont College in 1984. To be effective such a form must be comprehensive, flexible, comfortable for the counselor to use and easily adapted to the variety of clients seen by the counselor.[1]

The "Career/Life Profile and Planning Record" (Figures 3-1 through 3-4) as presented in this chapter can be used progressively throughout the entire counseling process from the initial interview through closure. It includes a section for all background information, space to record the client's goals, tests administered, notes from the counselor's observations, assignments, conclusions drawn and recommendations or suggestions. Most sections of this record are best written by the counselor as doing so provides the optimal oppor-

Figure 3-1 Intake Form: Career Life Profile and Planning Record

NAME _____ LAST _____ FIRST _____ Middle _____

REFERRED BY _____

FIRST VISIT _____ / _____ / _____ MONTH DAY year

OCCUPATION _____

CURRENT CAREER CHANGE: Being considered or in progress _____

CAREER/LIFE PROFILE AND PLANNING RECORD

NOTE: This is a confidential record of your history and will be kept in this office. Information contained herein will not be released to any person except upon your authorization.

This record is designed to aid in planning a successful career transition. Please answer every question to the best of your ability so that we may work together toward achieving your goals.

Ⓐ GENERAL INFORMATION

Address _____

Age _____

Sex _____

Telephone: Home ( ) _____ Work ( ) _____

Spouse's Name _____ Occupation _____

Marital Status   How Long?   Son or Daughter   Age   W/you   Occupation
Married ( )   Y N
Single ( )   Y N
Widowed ( )   Y N
Divorced ( )   Y N

Ⓑ

What motivated you to consider career counseling at this time? _____

Ⓒ

What do you hope to accomplish by coming to the Career and Life Planning Center? _____

Ⓓ FAMILY HISTORY

Father Living? Yes No

Mother Living? Yes No

Education _____ Occupation _____

Name   Age   Education   Occupation

Brother(s): _____

Sister(s): _____

Ⓔ EDUCATION

Please indicate highest educational level achieved and the year completed.

High School _____ College _____

Graduate School _____

Vocational Training/Other Course Work _____

Could you undertake more schooling at this time?   No   Yes

Ⓕ CAREER HISTORY

Please List Occupations   How Long?   Reason for leaving?

High School Jobs _____

College _____

Ⓖ ORGANIZATIONS

Please list organizations in which you have been involved (Professional, business, volunteer, cultural, social, political, etc.)

Organization   How Long?   Offices Held

Ⓗ HONORS

Please list any honors, awards or achievements in any of the areas mentioned above:

Career and Life Planning, Norma Zuber and Associates

34

Figure 3-2 Intake Form: Physical History and Personal/Career Needs and Objectives

PHYSICAL HISTORY (A)

Date of last physical examination ___/___/___

Physical condition:
( ) Poor   ( ) Good   ( ) Excellent

Height: _____
Weight: Now _____
One year ago _____
Ideal _____

Physical Disabilities or problems _____

Physician's name _____

Do You . . .	Circle one	Change in past 3 years?
Exercise	No Yes	
Smoke	No Yes	
Drink	No Yes	
Overeat	No Yes	
Have Loss of Appetite	No Yes	

Have You Had . . .	Circle one	Check if in last 2 year
Heart Disease	No Yes	
Arthritis	No Yes	
Anemia	No Yes	
Migraine Headaches	No Yes	
High or Low Blood Pressure	No Yes	
Asthma	No Yes	
Allergies	No Yes	

Do You Experience . . .		
Frequent or Severe Headaches	No Yes	
Fainting Spells	No Yes	
Eye Glasses	No Yes	
Recurrent Colds	No Yes	
Chest Pains	No Yes	
Night Sweats	No Yes	
Shortness of Breath on:		
Walking several blocks	No Yes	
Walking one flight of stairs	No Yes	
Recurrent Stomach Pain	No Yes	
Sleep Disruption	No Yes	
Digestive Problems	No Yes	
Muscle Spasms	No Yes	
Hot flashes	No Yes	
Tiredness Without Apparent Reason	No Yes	
Other _____		

(B) PERSONAL/CAREER NEEDS AND OBJECTIVES

What are your most urgent life concerns right now?
_____
_____

What are your most important career objectives?
_____
_____

Considering your financial responsibilities at this time, what would be a reasonable acceptable income for you? $ _____
_____

What are your greatest personal strengths?
_____
_____

What words or phrases would you or those who know you well (spouse, friends, co-workers) use to describe you?
_____
_____

What skills, hobbies or avocational interests do you have?
_____
_____

What have been the *most satisfying* aspects of your work situations? (These could relate to supervision, personnel, co-workers, tasks, work environment, salary or income, physical activity or responsibilities.)
_____
_____

What have been the *most dissatisfying* aspects of your work situations?
_____
_____

Career and Life Planning, Norma Zuber and Associates

35

Figure 3-3 Intake Form: Stress Factors and Feelings

STRESS FACTORS* (A)

Please mark any of the following factors which apply to you.

( ) New Marriage
( ) Divorce
( ) Separation from mate
( ) Reconciliation with mate
( ) Major change in number of spousal disagreements (regarding child rearing, personal habits, etc.)

Son or daughter leaving home:
( ) Under *positive* circumstances (marriage, college, etc.)
( ) Under *negative* circumstances

( ) Death of close family member
( ) Death of a close friend

( ) Major change in health or behavior of family member
( ) Pregnancy
( ) Gaining a new family member (through birth, marriage, oldster moving in)
( ) Responsibility for chronically ill person
( ) Problem relationship with in-laws
( ) Care or responsibility for ageing parent
( ) Major change in working hours, conditions or responsibilities (promotion, demotion, lateral transfer)
( ) Major business adjustment (merger, reorganization, bankruptcy, etc.)
( ) Change to different line of work
( ) Troubles with the boss
( ) Retirement from work
( ) Major change in financial state (significantly better or worse)

( ) Taking on a mortgage or significant financial commitment
( ) Major change in living conditions (new or deteriorating home)
( ) Change in residence
( ) Beginning or ceasing formal schooling
( ) Change to a new school
( ) Spouse beginning or ceasing work outside of home

( ) Outstanding personal achievement
( ) Death of spouse
( ) Revision of personal habits (dress, mannerisms, etc.)
( ) Major change in eating habits
( ) Sexual difficulties

( ) Catastrophic injury or illness
( ) Major change in usual type or amount of recreation or exercise
( ) Major change in social activities (increase or decrease)
( ) Major change in spiritual involvement
( ) Major change in number of family get-togethers

( ) Vacation
( ) Christmas
( ) Detention in jail or other institution
( ) Minor violations of the law (traffic ticket, etc.)
( ) Other _____

*Adapted from: Holmes, T., Life Situations, Emotions and Disease.
J. Acad. Med., 19:747, 1978

(B) FEELINGS

The next section will explore feelings you may have encountered through-out your life. The purpose of this exercise is to identify any current shifts or changes in your emotional well being.

Using the following scale, please circle the appropriate number:

Never 1
Decreased intensity within past year 2
About the same 3
Increased intensity within past year 4

Disappointment	1	2	3	4
Anger	1	2	3	4
Fear	1	2	3	4
Anxiety	1	2	3	4
Loneliness	1	2	3	4
Frustration	1	2	3	4
Anticipation	1	2	3	4
Depression	1	2	3	4
Hopelessness	1	2	3	4
Excitement	1	2	3	4
Confusion	1	2	3	4
Tension	1	2	3	4
Diminished self-worth	1	2	3	4
Despair	1	2	3	4
Happiness	1	2	3	4
Satisfaction	1	2	3	4
Sense of accomplishment	1	2	3	4
Guilt	1	2	3	4
Deeply disturbed	1	2	3	4
Others significant to you:				
	1	2	3	4
	1	2	3	4

Are you now in personal counseling (as well as career counseling)?   No   Yes
If yes, what are the reasons? _____

Is the spiritual component of your life satisfying?   No   Yes
Please elaborate _____

tunity for interchange, discussion and clarity through the process. Individual components of the "Career/Life Profile and Planning Record" will be illustrated and discussed throughout this chapter.

Since career and life issues are so integrally related, it is important to view the client as a whole and to adopt a balanced approach that addresses the individual's physical, emotional, intellectual, spiritual and social aspects as well as vocational concerns. The intake form should be viewed as a tool for discovering the uniqueness of each client. It is a very useful tool, but not to be used as a "fill-in-the-blank" rote to follow, or in a "cookie cutter" approach toward the client.

The counselor's relationship and connection with the client begins with the first encounter. Rapport can be established or damaged as interaction between the counselor and client begins. Intake begins at the first point of contact. It may take place on the telephone prior to

the first session or at the moment a person enters the counselor's office to start the career development process. Much can be observed in the first few seconds. Is the client's attitude open and positive, or is it one that is closed or hesitant? Are dress and grooming clean, coordinated and neat, or is the client's appearance hygienically or visually indifferent or poor. Attitudes and grooming habits may reflect confidence and maturity, or depression and low self-esteem, or possibly simply indicate the level of awareness and understanding of socially accepted standards the client possesses. Body language can also give clues. For example, the ability or inability to make eye contact or the person's posture may reveal confidence or insecurity. A message is conveyed in a firm or weak handshake. If the counselor identifies troublesome areas through these indicators, the problems may need to be confronted at an appropriate time such as in a practice job interview. The counselor might suggest community resources or workshops for the client to attend or appropriate books to read such as *Image Impact* (Thompson 1990). These observations and recommendations duly noted may be recorded on the intake form in the Comments section (Figure 3-4).

Figure 3-4 Intake Form: Tests Administered and Comments

COUNSELOR: _____

TESTS:

COMMENTS, ASSIGNMENTS AND ADVISING RECORD

ADMINISTERED	DATE	RESULTS	DATE

WORKSHOPS ATTENDED   FEE   PDN-PD   DATE

Resume Writing
Job Search
Decision Making
Interviewing Skills

COUNSELING SESSIONS   FEE _____

Career and Life Planning, Norma Zuber and Associates

General information about the client such as address, telephone number, current occupation, age, sex, referral source, etc. may be completed by the client outside the actual session or by the counselor at the outset of the first session. If, however, the counselor chooses to gather basic information through interviewing, this might be an excellent opportunity for the client to begin to relax, to observe the counselor and to feel more comfortable and at ease while providing non-threatening data.

It is appropriate to include a review of the process after the general information is gathered so that the client knows what to expect and misconceptions can be clarified. The extent and limits of confidentiality should also be stated at this point. The counselor can then present a step-by-step process for making appropriate career choices, establishing a career goal and developing a plan of action.

The gathering and recording of background information begins next. Such information will provide a comprehensive picture of the client's life, furnishing insights into work patterns, family and work relationships, social support systems, cultural or sociological influences, strengths, preferences, dreams and a number of other pieces of pertinent data. This knowledge can give the counselor insight into reasons for certain occupational choices or directions the client has followed in the past, or it can indicate where the client may be stuck because of fixed inaccurate work related beliefs.

In moving into the area of marital status, spouse's occupation, dependent and/or independent children and their ages and occupations (circle A, Figure 3-1), the counselor may uncover problems or constraints of a financial or personal nature such as the client being a single parent, having a retarded child or being in the midst of a divorce. All constraints are important in realistic career planning.

Circle B, Figure 3-1 identifies motivating factors or reasons a client seeks career guidance. It is important that the counselor is aware that the presenting problem may not be the true reason the client has initiated counseling. Life issues may surface at this time such as chronic dissatisfaction, struggles with authority, depression or neuroses. Since career counseling may carry a more positive connotation for the client than psychological counseling, a client may seek this form of counseling expecting that a perfect career will solve all of life's other problems. This may be the time to help the client separate such issues and to begin to find solutions. This may also be a good time to discuss the possible unreality of the expectation that a career change could be the sole answer to achieving happiness, security, peace, etc. A referral for therapy may be appropriate at this juncture.

Once the client's motivation and needs are identified and the counseling process is understood, a goal can be determined (circle C, Figure 3-1). Goals must be attainable, flexible and fall within the counselor's and the client's capabilities, competence and value systems. The goal is what the client wants to achieve from the process, such as, ''I would like to better understand myself and what I need from life or a career to be satisfied.'' Or, ''I need some clear career options and direction and some help in setting goals.'' The goal is stated and recorded on the form. It may be written down verbatim and any part that is unacceptable or that cannot be realistically achieved can be adjusted through the process of working with the client. Once the goal is established the direction of the process will be focused. The goal should be reviewed with the client periodically throughout the course of counseling to keep the process on target, to make revisions if necessary and to provide recognition when the goal has been achieved. Having a goal from the outset prevents the disappointment of wishful expectations which cannot be met.

A useful family history includes parents' education and occupations, the client's birth order, siblings' education and occupations, any attitudes and expectations imposed on the client during formative years, relationships and/or problems within the family. Such information which can be recorded in a form, such as shown at circle D on Figure 3-1, can provide clues which might indicate pressures shaping the client's motivations and work concepts. If these concepts are distorted or limiting they may need to be worked through in order for the client to make more enlightened choices.

Educational history, such as illustrated in Figure 3-1 circle E, consists of information indicating the highest level of schooling achieved and year attained, most successful and least successful courses or classes, grade point average, any vocational or technical courses and special skills or training. Also, the question of the client's willingness to undertake any further education or training needs to be addressed.

A career history (Figure 3-1, circle F) should not only reflect positions held, but terms of employment and reasons for leaving, as well. Frequent job changes or consistently negative reasons for leaving may highlight vocational patterns which need discussion and problem-solving. Jobs during high school may reveal early ambitions or the level of maturity during that period.

Reviewing organizations (Figure 3-1, circle G) in which a client has participated or is currently active may indicate transferable interest and skills which could be used in a paid occupation. In contrast, lack of participation in organizations could indicate a narrow focus, depression or withdrawal; or, it could simply reflect an introverted personality or heavy time constraints.

The section of the intake form on honors, awards and achievements (Figure 3-1, circle H) gives the client the opportunity to identify areas of excellence, e.g., sports, arts or academics, which have received public recognition as well as achievements which may not have received outside acknowledgment, but which are a source of pride or personal fulfillment for the client.

An overview of the client's physical history (Figure 3-2, circle A) can be covered even though the counselor's role is not that of a medical diagnostician. It is important that the counselor have enough skill and knowledge to identify and discuss possible physical problems which would preclude certain types of work as well as substance abuse, stress related symptoms, depression or any problems which might suggest the need for the client to be seen by a physician. A counselor with no medical background can gain enough awareness to recognize problems requiring attention or referral by learning from experts either through questioning in person or through reading. Books such as the *Layman's Guide to Medical Symptoms* (Rosenfeld, 1989) and *Symptom Analysis and Physical Diagnosis* (Davis, 1985) are excellent resources. Other areas of counselor awareness should include recognizing signs of learning disabilities (Salvia & Ysseldyke, 1991) or neurosis. A network of community resources for referrals is important to have at hand. Personal and career needs and objectives (Figure 3-2, circle B) provide life and career information from the client's perspective. Unless a client is somewhat introspective, answering these questions may be difficult. The counselor may introduce and explain this section and then have the client complete it as homework before the next session in order to give the client enough time to think it through. Counselor and client can then discuss the information in depth at their next meeting. Specific occupations, once targeted, can be filtered through the context of these subjective introspections and weighed to determine how appropriately they fit the client's needs and objectives.

The evaluation of stress factors and feelings may be more or less useful for certain specific clients and should be used at the counselor's discretion. These two exercises can be completed prior to a session or in a few minutes during a session.

Stress Factors (Figure 3-3, circle A) is an adapted list of life events (Holmes, 1978), with space to add events which may not be listed, but which may be particular to the specific client. Frequently, when a client can see a clear and sometimes startling list of stress factors a certain perspective is gained. Often undefined feelings of dissonance can be understood. As these events are reviewed and discussed during the session some may be alleviated through counseling or through referral to other resources.

The exercise on Feelings (Figure 3-3, circle B) is used to identify any current shift or changes in the client's emotional well being. A great deal of information can be gleaned from this simple exercise such as strong reactions to life circumstances, guilt over some event, "mid-life crisis" or excitement and anticipation over coming changes. If a client indicates the increased intensity of feeling "deeply disturbed" the counselor may, through questioning, discover pathology or mental distress which should be addressed, or some profound personal problem needing attention.

Following the exercise on feelings and personal stress are two questions. One is about therapeutic counseling and one is about the client's spiritual satisfaction. Personal counseling needs to be addressed in order to understand possible barriers to a successful, satisfying career choice. The career counselor should also be aware if the client is receiving psychogenic medication. It is often helpful to interact with the client's therapist. Since this type of conference relates to confidential information, an authorization releasing confidentiality must be signed by the client in order for the counselors to ethically and openly confer. In working together a therapist, career counselor and client frequently can arrive at more balanced options and solutions for the client.

The next question is about the spiritual aspect of the client's life. This particular element of the "whole" person may be another sensitive area for both counselor and client and should be approached only if the counselor is settled personally in this area and is comfortable discussing this subject with the client. There is an increasing awareness in the field of counseling and psychology that hunger for spirituality is growing and that the spiritual aspect of a client's life is a vital one. The counselor may see many clients with wounds in this area of life. The client may be stuck in high school or college attitudes about religion and spirituality imposed by rigid parents, churches or organizations. Or, the client may have found that a materialistic world view has not been satisfying and feel that there is a void.

The counselor must be alert and sensitive, honoring the uniqueness of each client whle encouraging the client to discover what specific step toward spiritual development would be helpful. The steps might include reading, rethinking or discussing these issues with some particular resource. The counselor must be especially careful not to manipulate or influence the client into the counselor's world view at this possibly vulnerable time with a "soup kitchen" attitude.

It is useful for the counselor to have succinct, detailed, dated records of tests administered, workshops attended, payments of fees, dates and content of sessions, as well as comments, advising or assigned homework (Figure 3-4). Such records can be used as a quick and accurate review for the counselor. Accurate records are also important in case of any legal action. However, discretion must be exercised by the counselor in regard to the advisability of recording particularly sensitive or personal information that has a bearing on the career counseling process and that could be considered "privileged" between counselor and client.

Information for the client on the career counseling process and the counselor's credentials and abilities are necessary in order to protect the counselor, to facilitate clarity for the client and to avoid any misunderstanding. It is most helpful to provide printed information reinforcing prior verbal descriptions and explanations. This is best done at the end of the first session. To affirm the credentials and credibility of the counselor and to restate the services offered for career development, the *Consumer Guidelines For Selecting A Career Counselor,* published by the National Career Development Association as shown in Chapter 7, Figure 7-7, is an excellent piece of information for the client.

A clear statement of policies (Figure 3-5) prevents any misunderstanding about office procedures. This statement should cover the counselor's policies on appointments, testing, fees, confidentiality or any other areas unique or important to the counselor's practice. At the beginning of the subsequent session the counselor may ask if the client (or the client's parents in the case of a dependent minor) has any questions or comments.

The intake and information portion of the career counseling process should usually be completed in one or two sessions including the outside assignments. Intake must be systematic and thorough in order to be effective, but it must also be a flexible process which is sensitive to the client. The counselor must be careful not to allow the structure of the intake to overpower the needs and uniqueness of the client, or to make the process mechanical or arbitrary in any way.

This chapter has presented one method as a possible guideline for a counselor establishing a procedure for intake. It is not intended for adoption, as a whole, as each counselor must develop a personal technique which is not only comprehensive, but also comfortable and fitted to the counselor's personal style.

Boggs, Johnson, et. al. (1982). *Discovery.* Minneapolis: Introspective Scoring Systems.

Davis, A. (1985). *Symptom analysis and physical diagnosis.* New York: MacMillan Publishing Company.

Holmes, T. (1978). *Life situations, emotions and disease. J. Acad. Med., 19,* 747.

Rosenfeld, I. (1989). *Layman's guide to medical symptoms.* New York: Simon and Schuster.

Salvia, J. & Ysseldyke, J. (1987). *Assessment* (5th ed.) p. 586. Boston: Houghton & Mifflin.

Thompson, J. (1990). *Image impact.* New York: Bristol Books.

Yost, E. & Corbishley, M.A. (1987). *Career counseling, A Psychological approach.* San Francisco: Jossey-Bass, Inc.

Figure 3-5   Statement of Policies

STATEMENT OF POLICIES

We are pleased that you have chosen to use our services for your career and life planning. We look forward to the successful completion of your goals as we move, with you, through this effective process!

In order to prevent misunderstandings about office procedures, testing or billing we would like for you to have a clear statement about how and why we function as we do.

APPOINTMENTS are generally one hour and fifteen minutes in length and are scheduled once a week. These may be scheduled Tuesday through Friday from 7:30 am to 5:00 pm or on Saturday mornings. However, depending on your concerns, sessions may be scheduled more or less frequently. The number of sessions needed varies with each person so this may need to be a point of discussion. If you need to cancel an appointment please notify us 24 hours in advance, otherwise there is a $45.00 charge for missed appointments.

TESTS may be taken in a group with two to seven others from 9:00 to 12:00 on Friday mornings at a cost of 120.00 for the full battery or 40.00 per hour if only one or two instruments are used. Should you prefer another time these can be administered during a regular session for the regular session fee.

Tests are administered by a qualified person according to the specific requirements and guidelines of the various publishing companies from whom they are obtained. These guidelines prevent us from ethically selling these instruments or allowing them to be taken without professional administration and supervision.

FEES are 85.00 for the 75 minute session. Payment is generally made at each appointment. If you would prefer being billed on a monthly basis or at the termination of services we will gladly set up a payment plan. However, there is a finance charge of 2 percent on your unpaid balance for accounts carried over 30 days. Under certain circumstances these fees are tax deductible, so you may want to consult your accountant.

CONFIDENTIALITY is strictly maintained unless you issue a written release. Exceptions of confidentiality include:

1)   Possible need for consultation with another professional, without using your name, unless you request otherwise.

2)   If you make a statement of intent to harm yourself or others we are required by law to do anything we feel is necessary to prevent this occurrence.

3)   If you have participated in a crime or are planning to do so, legally we are required to inform the proper authorities.

THE CAREER AND LIFE PLANNING process is an exciting one! You will gain perspective as to how your own personal attributes, needs and objectives will best fit with appropriate occupational choices. Goals will be developed to reach your desired objectives. The process requires active participation on your part with the completion of outside assignments which will provide needed information to make the most effective decisions. Although career development is a comprehensive process you may terminate at any point paying only for services received. We look forward to working with you and proceed with the assumption that you have read and are in agreement with our policies. If you have any reservations, questions or suggestions, please discuss these with your counselor.

44

Chapter Four — Psychological Aspects of Career Counseling

Mary-Lynne Musgrove
Musgrove Career Counseling
Columbus, OH

Last summer we conducted a small study in our career counseling practice. We administered the Structured Interview for DSM-IIIR Personality (SIDP-R) (Pfohl et. al., 1989) to 44 clients and found that 18% of them met full criteria for one or more personality disorders. The number of subjects in this study was too small and the methodology too casual to make generalizations, but the study does raise an important question for career counselors: What is the effect

of personality pathology on career development and the process of career counseling?

Steve Hampl, one of my colleagues, gives an example of a client diagnosed as a paranoid personality. It is quite likely that the paranoid's interpersonal sensitivity and projection of blame will result in less than satisfying work adjustment. Indeed, this particular client had quit several jobs because he believed he was being treated unfairly. A counselor who is unaware of the underlying personality disturbance may unwittingly accept the client's attribution of blame to the external interpersonal environment. A counselor in this position may work too quickly to facilitate a career transition, perhaps failing to recognize that the work adjustment problem is a function of ongoing, self-generated strife rather than a genuine incongruence between client and career (Hampl, Musgrove, and Carmin, 1990).

Further, we found that the self-report measures used in the study generally failed to discriminate personality disordered from non-personality disordered clients. We concluded that standard assessment instruments often used in career counseling may not be useful

The material in this chapter was originally developed for the JFK University Career Development Summer Institute, 1989.

for indicating personality disturbance. These issues need to be addressed on a broad scale in our field of career counseling. Most career counselors have a minimum number of courses in psychological diagnostics and assessment, and too often the coursework focuses on test administration and interpretation. The result is that many counselors provide career services in good faith but then cannot explain why the client does not complete the process, or fails to implement change, or repeats the problem in the next job.

The solution does not seem to lie in just taking more courses in psychology, for many who are heavily trained in that field still find the particular permutations found in career counseling to be thorny — even to the point that they assess career counseling to be more difficult to do than psychotherapy (Hampl, 1990).

Meanwhile, vocational theory does not give us a framework for understanding the relationship of psychological and vocational issues, nor does it provide us with a career counseling model which will help us frame what we are seeing in the counseling room. It seems that the solution lies in our developing a framework ourselves which will reflect the relationship of psychological and vocational issues and which will guide our practice as career counselors.

In this chapter I would like to briefly outline a vocational theory and career counseling model and to show how the model can be implemented in practice. Both the theory and the model are only a beginning definition of the psychological/vocational connection, and I offer them as a place to start and invite you as practitioners to improve on this beginning and to start to develop theory yourselves.

The history of vocational theory has largely been a history of trying to describe the determinants that affect vocational behavior. (For example, Roe described the involuntary, non-psychological determinants; Holland described personality determinants; Brill described sublimation determinants; Super stated that the stage of life development is a determinant and that self concept is a determinant, etc.) For career counselors, it may be more useful to change the question that we have been asking for the past 70 years — change it from, "What factors in development influence a person's career choice," to "What factors *interfere* with the normal process of vocational development?"

And so the central postulate of my theory stands on a concept little researched but long known by vocational psychologists — that vocational development is a normal developmental process — and seeks to understand the factors that interfere with this process.

Theory

The postulate and corollaries are these:

Central Postulate: Vocational development is a normal

46

developmental process.

Construction Corollary: Individuals who have had normal physical, mental, and emotional development will choose work that is satisfying and interesting to them.

Reverse Corollary: Individuals who have had significant physical, mental, or emotional barriers to normal development will experience difficulty in choosing and implementing work that is satisfying and interesting to them.

Thinking/Environment Corollary: Individuals who have had normal physical, mental, and emotional development but who develop significant thinking errors, or who encounter significant environmental barriers, will also experience difficulty in choosing and implementing work that is satisfying and interesting to them.

> Examples of cognitive errors: "I won't be able to do anything to improve my career satisfaction because I don't have an education." (or) "I have to go into teaching because it's the only thing that will fit my children's schedules."

> In environmenal barriers, I also include what I call "situational barriers" — people overwhelmed with grieving in divorce or loss; those in extreme fatigue — as well as sex, race and age barriers.

Resolution Corollary: When the barriers are removed, the individual will be able to choose and implement work that is satisfying and interesting.

Model for Career Counseling

The model for career counseling which is built on this theory is shown in Figure 4-1.

This can be viewed as a picture of the client. At the vocational center of the client is his or her own internal job description, the heart of which is the place where gifts and fascinations meet. The dotted lines around the center show the physical/mental/emotional/thinking/environmental barriers which make it difficult for the client to find and implement the internal job description. The arrows pointing toward the center denote that there are some barriers that block the client's knowing what the internal job description is; the arrows pointing away from the center denote that there are also barriers which block implementing the internal job description once it is located.

On the one hand, it would seem that all we would need to do, when a new client comes to see us, is to tap the radiant center by testing the person or by doing some exercises. But with large numbers of people who come to see us, we find that it is not that easy. Instead, we find

Figure 4-1   Model of Career Counseling Process

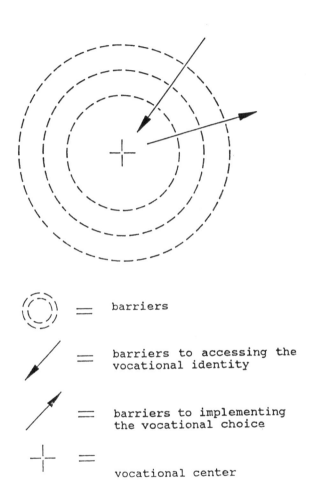

barriers

barriers to accessing the
vocational identity

barriers to implementing
the vocational choice

vocational center

people who do not seem "motivated," who seem "lazy" or "afraid to take life in hand" — or that the person has a "flat interest profile."

I believe that what we are actually seeing are the things that the theory speaks of — the physical, mental, emotional, thinking, or environmental barriers to normal vocational development. Let me give some examples:

> *Alice* — She is kinesthetic, artistic, creative, and original. She absolutely does not see it. She is in full denial of it. Why? Because she dislikes herself so much that she cannot allow herself to embrace her own radiance.
>
> *Carl* — I could see at the outset that he is a natural salesman. But he has sabotaged himself in every job that he has had — because his "adult child of alcoholics" background has created such guilt in him that he cannot allow himself to enact his own identity.
>
> *Grace* — She is a gifted writer, art historian and researcher. A true academic. She has not allowed herself to get a college education — because she was sexually abused as a child and carries remorse, guilt and anger.

What am I saying here? That one major barrier to seeing and embracing one's identity comes from guilt and childhood trauma. So here we have the person with a fully developed internal job description — and the owner of it unable to see it! It is not that the job description is lacking — or even that we as outsiders cannot spot it — but we have the problem of the person having an astigmatism caused by the warping of his/her life by childhood trauma.

Is trauma from childhood the only barrier to the center? No, I also can immediately think of others:

—strong societal messages regarding proper role,
—physical or mental disabilities,
—early onset of alcoholism or drug abuse, and
—serious sibling rivalry.

I have not named yet all of the barrier classifications to vocational identity, but for working purposes have collapsed them into physical, mental, emotional, thinking, and environmental/situational barriers.

The Work of the Career Counselor

The role of the counselor is to identify and help remove the barriers. I believe that the work of the career counselor occurs in six stages:

Stage I. ASSESSMENT. The counselor conducts psychological assessment *(not treatment)* early in the career counseling process in

49

order to determine with the client whether there are barriers that are blocking access to vocational identity. I believe that this is a critical step in career counseling. We simply cannot serve our clients well when we go through a short introductory process and then begin assessing vocational interests. By the time that we are sufficiently expert in this work to be in private practice, we must be expert in psychological diagnostics.

In practice, we conduct psychological assessment by doing several things concurrently. We take a Gestaltist's view by closely observing non-verbal behavior which reveals depression, nervousness, low self-esteem, disorientation, etc. We take a social work/systems view by inquiring about all of the systems which currently impact the person (presenting situation socioeconomic level, physical, mental, educational, mental, financial, social, marital situations). We take a developmentalist's view by assessing the history of relationships in the family of origin. We take a cognitivist's view by observing cognitive errors and observing the structure of the language used by the client.

If what we find, as we do this assessment, is that there seem to be no major barriers, then we ask ourselves, "Just what has kept this person from finding and implementing his/her vocational identity?" Sometimes we find that the internal job description is very complex; sometimes we find that the person is simply young or inexperienced; sometimes we find that the person only needs information or a sounding board. Then we move to our usual vocational assessment and find that our work moves quite smoothly. But where we do find major barriers, we then must move to Stage II of our work.

Stage II. BARRIERS ARE ADDRESSED. The counselor's behavior becomes differentiated based on the assessment: (a) serious unresolved issues from childhood which block access are referred to a psychotherapist (or treated by the career counselor if that person is legally qualified to treat mental/emotional disorders); (b) cognitive errors are addressed by the counselor; (c) situational barriers are examined by the counselor and client to assess whether they preclude continuation of the career counseling process. I believe that doing Stage I and Stage II work is what distinguishes the successful, experienced private practitioner from the less successful and inexperienced private practitioner.

Stage III. VOCATIONAL IDENTITY IS EXPLORED. We now move into the purest part of career counseling — the exploration of the person's vocational identity. And what we find is that underneath the barriers, underneath the resulting lack of articulation, the client *knows* who she or he is and exactly what the internal job description is. She or he just does not know that she or he knows it. At the center is a complete and accurate job description (not just one job title) waiting to be spoken. At Stage III, our work is easy. We can create all kinds of things, use any tools, design anything that comes to our mind that will help the person tell us the whole job description. I will not linger over this since so much has been written and taught on this part of the work.

Stage IV. EXIT BARRIERS ARE ASSESSED. The moment that the internal job description is spoken, the vocational center declared, the barriers to implementing the career choice begin to emerge. These are: (a) resistance to change itself; (b) remaining psychodynamic barriers, which play an encore now; and (c) cognitive errors.

Every career counselor has encountered multiple examples of client failure to implement career choices that are "right" from every angle. There is often a high dropout rate in the career counseling process at the very moment that the client should be able to enjoy implementing the hard-won choice.

What happens to the internal processes of the client at this point may best be explained by integrating perspectives from psychodynamic theory, from Gestalt psychology, and from cognitive/behavioral therapy. More precisely, Gestalt psychology provides the framework for understanding the nature and handling of resistances; psychodynamic theory provides information about the content (subject) of many resistances; and cognitive/behavioral therapy adds further content areas and suggest interventions that can be integrated with the Gestalt interventions.

Gestalt psychology teaches that for every force for change there is an opposite force for sameness. And within the force for sameness there is a wisdom. We need to then listen to the wisdom of the resistance. What does it teach? We can also work on resistance to change itself in accordance with Watzlawick, Weakland, and Fisch (1974): that the most powerful tool for change that they have found is paradox. So at the moment that the client is flogging him/herself toward implementation, we encourage him/her to slow down.

Stage V. EXIT BARRIERS ARE ADDRESSED. The psychodynamic factors that linger at this stage are re-assessed and one of two things happen: the client is referred to a therapist for further work, or the psychodynamic factors are now at a counseling level and are worked in the career counselor's office. An example of a thinking error at this stage: "I had a friend who tried to get into the field and she couldn't get a job in it, so I have to choose something else."

In the final stage of the work, we move to the normal career counseling techniques of job search.

Stage VI. JOB SEARCH. Finally, the career counselor becomes coach — teaching job search methodology, revising resumes, videotaping interview rehearsals. The career counselor is immensely practical here. We as counselors go from being the least practical person in the room (while exploring the ideal job) to being the most practical person in the room. And so our work comes to a close.

Work adjustment issues, not addressed here, usually precede or succeed other vocational work and need to be addressed separately unless they are symptoms of psychological issues.

As career counselors, we can develop a list of researchable questions related to the theories and models that we develop (a first question on my theory would be to find an operational definition of "normal"). With our clients' cooperation and permission, we can establish databases of information on your private practice clients and can do studies that will contribute to the literature in our field. As practitioners, we are in a unique role to affect the theory/research/practice interplay, and I hope that you will turn your case note writing into material to teach the rest of us.

Hampl, S., Musgrove, T., & Carmin, C. (1990)."Personality disorders among adult career clients." Poster paper presented at the annual meeting of the American Psychological Association, Boston.

Hampl, S. (1990). "Adult career counseling is not a trivial activity." Poster paper presented at the annual meeting of the American Psychological Association, Boston.

Pfohl, B., Blum, N., Zimmerman, M., & Stangl, D. (1989). *Structured interview for DSM III R personality.* Iowa City, IA: University of Iowa College of Medicine.

Watzlawick, P., Weakland, J. and Fisch, R. (1974). *Change.* New York: W. W. Norton.

Chapter Five — Selecting and Integrating Assessment into a Private Practice

Diane Shepard
Department of Human Services
University of North Carolina
at Charlotte

The career counseling process moves through a series of stages: an intake phase, a client self-assessment phase, a career and educational information phase and a job search phase. Effective decision-making and goal-setting skills, which include the abilities to compromise and change with change, are taught and reinforced throughout this process.

Many career counselors view testing as an independent function rather than as an integral part of this career counseling process. Because of this mind set, they tend to focus on identifying an appropriate instrument(s) based upon the perceived client's needs, the cost of the instruments, or the graduate training they received using selected insruments.

This chapter suggests a process that career counselors can use to select the type of testing they will make available to clients in their private practice. A model is presented for selecting a battery of tests and choosing the specific instruments in that battery.

In actuality, counselors should first identify their personal style of counseling based upon an eclectic theoretical approach. Style of counseling should then influence the design of a counseling process. After identifying the process, the counselor's theoretical approaches should then match the theoretical basis of the testing which will be available for clients. Then, based upon an assessment of client needs, the most appropriate instrument(s) for each individual client are chosen.

Because they do not go through this systematic method for selecting assessment instruments, career counselors often question which tests they should use, but not how to integrate the results into the counseling process represents the personal judgement each counselor must make when selecting the type of assessment and the actual instrument(s).

A Developmental Perspective On Career Assessment

Formal, standardized testing and informal testing can be integrated through a variety of media, such as interviews, written tests, computerized systems, or audiovisual formats into *each phase* of the career counseling process. Because trait-factor methods have historically dominated career counseling, many clinicians were trained to think of testing as a part of the self-assessment phase only in order to verify or identify individual characteristics. That self-information was then used to match a client to one or more jobs which required that particular set of characteristics.

Present day career counselors are more developmental in their approach than those in the past. They realize that clients may elect several career directions in their lifetimes. These changes are influenced by clients' present life situations, which may demand change and compromise in clients' original short and long term goals.

Counselors who accept this developmental approach usually feel that the decisions made during these changing life situations should not be made impulsively. Therefore, they choose a decision-making theory which explains *how* a person actually makes a choice and *what information* is needed to make effective choices.

Over time, people narrow down choice options by gradually processing psychological and occupational information. Gelatt's (1962) paradigm for decision-making has proved very useful in conceptualizing this process. This theoretical approach stresses the need for a predictive system (based upon knowledge of aptitude and career information), a valuing system (based upon knowledge of psychological needs) and a decision system.

Assessment is used to assure that the client has appropriate self-information based upon current self-expectations to plug into the predictive and valuing systems. This aids the client in making a more effective career decision, based upon personal characteristics. Such applications of assessment information to the decision-making process are made throughout the counseling process.

Intake Phase

During the intake phase, it is important to begin to gather client background data in order to design a counseling process which will meet client needs. Two types of testing which may be used during this phase are learning styles/disability testing and career maturity inventories.

As stated above, testing should be used throughout the career counseling process to aid in more effective decision-making. For example, during the intake phase a counselor may use assessment to detect learning disabilities. Clients will be faced with reading information throughout the counseling process; therefore, it is a good idea for the career counselor to be aware of any learning disabilities which will affect the client's processing of career-related reading material, whether it be a test, a computerized career information system, or written materials.

Another important factor to consider is the client's learning style. Learning style refers to the consistent way a person responds to and uses, or learns about, stimuli in the environment. Through research in cognitive learning, McKenny and Keen (1974) discovered that clients with particular learning styles tend to choose careers which will allow them to use the skills identified with that learning style.

For example, perceptive thinkers on the Myers-Briggs Type Indicator watch for cues in data, jump from one (the + part of data) to another searching for relationships, and then use those relationships in problem-solving. The researchers found that clients who demonstrated these types of learning skills enjoyed working as marketing executives, psychologists, or historians.

The learning style of the client is also important in order to choose interventions which will be appropriate. These interventions can include reading about careers, writing resumes and cover letters, or informational interviewing with professionals in careers.

If a client has experienced difficulty in an academic setting or has a physical handicap, that client should be referred as soon as possible in the counseling process to an appropriate agency or educational institution for learning disability or learning style assessment. A release of information form may be obtained so that the career counselor can receive and review the results of such testing with the specialist who is interpreting the results. One should also keep in mind that some clients require special testing conditions due to handicaps or learning style difficulties.

For example, the author once worked with a client who expressed no interest in and, in fact, was very hesitant about taking the testing recommended for him at the end of the intake session. Upon further discussion, it was discovered that he had been ridiculed and labeled as dumb by several of his teachers; therefore, he left school after completing the eighth grade.

He was encouraged to obtain testing for learning disabilities at the local community college. He was assessed as dyslexic. This learning disability had not been discovered in his school years. Upon the recommendation of the reading specialist, a test administrator read questions on any test selected for the self-assessment process of career counseling. He was sent on informational interviews with career professionals rather than have him going through a computerized system which required a high comfort level with reading. National data about careers were discussed with him to balance the information he received from local professionals.

The relationship he established with the reading specialist at the local community college was extremely important. She encouraged him to explore various technical training programs which would prepare him for the careers he was investigating as part of the career counseling process. She set up a special study program, which would support the client if he decided to pursue a technical degree.

Career Maturity Inventories

The intake phase is an appropriate time to assess the career maturity of clients. Developmentally, career counseling clients are probably in a state of transition, which will call for decisions to be made as they accomplish the necessary life tasks in that transition. A career maturity inventory measures the rate and progress clients have made through these developmental stages and how that compares to the rate and progress made by their peers.

As an example, adolescents and adults are the populations who seek career counseling through the author's private practice. Therefore, the Adult Career Concerns Inventory, by D.E. Super and others is most frequently used to assess career maturity. This instrument determines how planful clients are about careers and identifies concerns clients may have with accomplishing the developmental tasks at various life stages. This instrument is used to diagnose clients' career maturity level and to select interventions which will further enhance that developmental progress.

Self Assessment Phase

During the intake phase, the career maturity inventory and the intake interview may suggest that clients need to verify or identify individual characteristics to use during the decision-making process. Based upon a trait-factor theoretical orientation, counselors may choose to lead the client through a self-assessment phase using formal or informal testing.

The theoretical orientations of counselors should dictate the testing they choose to use during this phase. The author will use her own self to exemplify the influence of theoretical orientation on the selection of assessment tools.

The first psychological factor to consider during the self-assessment phase is personality. Developmentalists, such as Super, Starishesky, Matlin, and Jordaan (1963) emphasize the importance of self-concept in career decision-making. Psychological approaches, as developed by Holland, Roe, Adler, and Freud, agree that intrinsic motivations, which help to shape and then are expressed through personality characteristics, are the most important factor in making a vocational choice.

These theorists disagree on the amount and the degree of interaction that heredity and social factors have upon the development of unconscious or conscious needs and drives. They also disagree on the ages at which these factors begin to influence the development of these motivational factors and how they become active in making appropriate occupational choices. They do agree, however, that personality characteristics are important influences in the development of intrinsic needs and motivators.

Personality inventories help to identify needs and drives, as expressed through the client's self-concept or personality characteristics.

The author uses the Myers-Briggs Type Indicator (MBTI) to assess personality characteristics. The MBTI is based upon the personality theory of Carl Jung. He states that apparent random variation in behavior is actually quite consistent and based upon the way individuals use perception (become aware of stimuli) and judgement (come to conclusions about what they perceive).

These MBTI results enable me to stimulate clients to talk about their current feelings of satisfaction and dissatisfaction with job tasks, people relationships formed through the job, and feelings about the work site environment. This leads to a discussion of what needs are or are not being met in the current job and a decision of whether or not it is the work environment versus the career that is actually leading to the basic dissatisfactions.

For example, a 30 year old client sought career counseling after receiving a three month notice on his latest job. Six years ago, through a prison work release program, he obtained his first job in a large corporate electronics training program. In three years he progressed through several promotions. He was transferred to a new division of the company under a female manager, who had recently been hired into the company. Within six months he was fired by this manager for unauthorized use of a company vehicle.

He then obtained a position in a warehouse of another large company. Within three years, he had progressed to assistant warehouse manager. His manager was replaced at this time with a new female manager, younger than himself. Within six months, she had given him the current three month notice. She based her decision to replace him on the fact that he had developed a bad attitude. He sought career counseling, for he felt he was not in "the right career".

The MBTI described his preference as "Introvert, Sensing, Thinking, Judging (ISTJ)". These types are described as quiet, serious, and dependable. They are patient with detail and can handle detailed figures. They are very sensitive to criticism. They may have difficulty in responding to the feeling needs of others for they make their own decisions in an impersonal and rational manner. They are attracted to careers in production, construction, accounting, business, or other technical fields.

During the discussion of the results he stated that he really enjoyed the technical skills he used as assistant warehouse manager. The manual skill related-tasks also interested and satisfied him. He expressed no desire at this time to up-grade the high school education and on-the-job electronics training through formal training. He did state that he did not want to lose the company benefits he had acquired. He also enjoyed the respect and prestige he felt he had in a managerial position.

The MBTI results supported his statements about enjoying an environment which would allow him to use manual and technical skills. Therefore, the counselor focused upon the client's personality characteristics which had an impact on his communication and interpersonal relationship skills. Through this discussion, he realized that the relationships with his manager and several of his supervisors were more the source of his dissatisfaction than the job or career-related tasks he was performing. The problems created by these interpersonal relationships led to the development of his "bad attitude."

Further counseling sessions focused on improving the client's communication and interpersonal skills. Because of the relationship that had developed between himself and the supervisor, the client realized he had to leave his current department. He began to investigate opportunities within his current company and with other employers.

He was given the opportunity by his present employer to transfer to the printing department, which had a different line of management. He could choose to enter a training program which emphasized the use of manual skills. There was potential for him to eventually move into a supervisory position.

Although he felt unsure of his communication skills as a supervisor, he felt he would like to become a supervisor again. After searching for jobs with other employers, seeking information about transferring within his present company, and discussing all options with the counselor, the client stated that he felt the in-house training program in printing was the most feasible prospect. It would allow him sufficient time to learn, through continued counseling, the communication and interpersonal skills that would be necessary to become more successful in a supervisory position, while allowing him to keep present company benefits. Therefore, he choose to transfer to the printing department.

Interest Inventories

A second psychological factor that influences career choice is individual interests. According to Bodoin, Nachmann and Seigel (1963) certain occupations satisfy specific needs that are related to interests. John Holland (1973) stated that career choice is an extension of personality into the world of work, followed by subsequent acceptance (interest) or rejection (lack of interest) in specific occupational settings which attract specific occupational stereotypes. In other words, personality characteristics may well influence interests in certain occupational areas.

This statement has not been proven or disproven to date through research. Clinical experience suggests to the author that pesonality characteristics may indeed influence interest development. It seems apparent that significant others and the race, age, sex and the occupational stereotypes of clients about certain jobs can influence interest development.

Take for example, a young man who had received a bachelor's degree in human services. Immediately upon graduation, he accepted his first job in a human services agency as a case worker.

After a year in his "helping others" job, he entered career counseling because he had lost all interest in his job. The counselor administered the Myers-Briggs Type Indicator and the Strong Interest Inventory. His MBTI type was "ISTJ". The three areas of highest interest, in order of highest to lowest scores on the SII, were social, realistic, and conventional.

Background information gathered over several sessions indicated that both of his parents and several of his aunts and uncles were involved in "helping others" careers. In fact, he grew up in a household where many homeless people, or other transients (such as adolescent runaways) who were down on their luck, were invited to stay as long as needed. The messages he perceived from the significant others in his life seemed to direct him into a human services profession where he would be involved with directly helping others.

It was also discovered during the discussions of the test results, that he had taken a business minor during his degree program. He had really enjoyed his marketing classes and had actually done an internship in a human services agency, working in the administrative office and using his marketing and business-related skills.

This client stated that he was very unhappy in his job for he was expected to constantly help other people resolve their problems. He felt that his parents would be appalled if they heard him make that statement. They could never accept the fact that he much preferred to work with facts and figures than people.

If he had felt he had a choice, he would have majored in business in college. In fact, he had discussed changing majors with his parents from human services to business administration, but they had flatly refused to help him finance his education if he made that change. They felt a business-related career was a reflection of greed.

Although his strongest area of interest on the SII was social, it was evident throughout the counseling sessions that this client was not interested in helping others directly. His expressed interest in helping others on the SII may have been influenced by the values his significant others held. The expressed interest in working with facts and figures may have been influenced by personality characteristics.

Future counseling sessions enabled the client to decide which area, human services or business, would meet his personal needs. He decided to return to college and complete the necessary course work to apply for a graduate degree in business. He was planning to use the coursework to explore marketing, accounting, or health care planning/administration as possible areas of interest. He also discussed ways to approach his significant others with his decision. He began to search for work environments in which he could use business-related skills and still satisfy his value for contributing to society.

Applying Holland's theoretical orientation, the author chose an assessment instrument which uses Holland's typology to compare an individual's interests with the interests of satisfied workers in occupational settings. The Strong Interest Inventory (SII). The publishers of this test have done considerable work in trying to eliminate the sex-biased items, have created new scales so that both sexes may be evaluated on all scales, and have rewritten occupational titles in order to be gender neutral. I realize that there are still many unanswered questions concerning sex bias in interest inventories; however, I try to counteract the age, sex and occupational biases through my interpretation.

Since one of the basic differences in most interest inventories is the classification system used to report results, there is no need to use more than one interest inventory for each individual client. (See editor's comment at the end of this chapter.) The work classification system should be chosen by the career counselor based upon the process through which he/she intends to lead the client. Clients should not have to learn several different classification systems. This could actually lead to a great deal of confusion for clients, as they may focus on learning the classification system rather than on the interrelationship between interests and career choice.

Values Inventories

Values represent a third psychological factor which influences career choice. Most theorists agree that at an early age an individual internalizes values concerning work itself and the rewards that work is perceived to offer that individual. Martin Katz (1973) proved that the values one holds are clearly a determinant of career choice; therefore, it is necessary to assess clients' value priorities.

In some cases, the results of a values clarification exercise or test measurement will reflect clients' hierarchial structure accurately. However, in my clinical experience, I have seen many clients struggling with a discrepancy between the values they held before the current transitional period and the values they are beginning to express during their formation of a new life structure.

For example, a 30 year old business executive felt the need to acquire material possessions as a show of her success; therefore, the value of high income was given highest priority and job/career decisions were based on this value as highest priority. Recently, this executive had a baby.

She was offered a promotion to a vice president position, which would require a great deal of travel and time away from home. She realized she needed to clarify if family and leisure time were becoming more important values than high income. After going through a values clarification exercise, she found her priorities had indeed shifted. The counseling sessions then focused upon the options of accepting the position, seeking a new position, or changing her career focus.

The computerized SIGI PLUS system is especially helpful for values clarification and assessment. In the Self-Assessment Subsection of this system, clients prioritize current values, then play a game which helps them to recognize discrepancies between what they used to want and what they now want from a job or a career.

In the Location subsection, they begin to learn which careers will offer them the values they have just reprioritized. The computer printout allows the counselor to initiate discussion with the client about the value priority changes. This leads to further counseling sessions in which the focus is on the compromise, risk, and rewards of the career options generated by the computer.

The results of the SIGI PLUS values clarification activities and the discussions generated through them will give the client sufficient knowledge to use in the value prediction phase of the decision-making process. For example, the young executive discussed above went through the prediction system and valuing system in Gelatt's (1962) paradigm, using the self-information gained through the results of the MBTI, SII, and SIGI PLUS. She decided, after a joint counseling session with her spouse, to accept the vice president position for a "trial" time of a year. If the job required too much time away from the family, the executive would reassess the situation and make a possible change in job environments.

Skills Inventories

A fourth type of assessment which may be used in the self assessment phase concerns skills. Most clients become aware of their skills and abilities as they use them in formal or informal academic training and work experience.

People acquire skills in very unique ways, specific to their individual personality characteristics and life situations. Career/job skills may be categorized as functional (transferable), self management (work attitude and habit) and work content (job specific). There are many techniques that can be used to improve the learning of these skills once an assessment is made.

There are a variety of reasons to assess skills before making a career decision. For example, if clients have received an injury which will prevent use of skills already learned, they may need to assess the potential for developing new skills. Another reason may be to support what clients already know about their skills, but perhaps may doubt because of a negative work experience or burn out. It also may be necessary to allow clients to take a skills assessment if they feel that they have a secondary set of skills that they have not yet discovered or used within their current job/career.

For example, one client was very talented in music and, because of this exceptional talent, worked solely as a performer in an orchestra. He felt burned out in music, however, and wanted to identify another set of skills which could be used to make a career change. After going through a skills assessment, the client realized his interest in organizational and management skills and began to explore careers related to management.

The skills assessment subsection of SIGI PLUS helps one identify functional skills which, can be transferred into new career directions. Clients have been reinforced throughout their lives in a variety of life situations for the skills they have developed. Sometimes the reinforcement has been positive; therefore, they continue to use and improve upon those skills. In other cases, they have been reinforced negatively for learning certain skills; therefore, they discontinue the use of those skills.

Based upon this behavioral principle, I feel that clients' self-perceptions about their skills can be valid. I encourage clients to consider trying out new skills which they may not have used before. If appropriate, I also encourage clients to try out a skill they may have used once, but were reinforced negatively for using. They may not have been placed in a life situation in which these skills have been evaluated accurately and without prejudice. That does not mean they may not be able to learn or enjoy the use of these skills.

For example, a client had a one day experience as a substitute teacher in a middle grades school. The experience was not pleasant because of many discipline problems in the classroom. Based upon that one day, he stated he was not at all interested in teaching.

After reviewing the skill assessment results of the SIGI PLUS system, he realized that he could demonstrate to others how to perform manual skills. In fact, he was so skilled at teaching others the "how to's" of auto mechanics, that he had been chosen as the unofficial "trainer" for all apprentice mechanics at the dealership where he worked. He had not recognized training adults as a form of "teaching." The list of careers generated in the SIGI PLUS system suggested teaching-related fields as one area for exploration.

After investigating many career areas, he chose to use the teaching skills he valued with a student population which would require less disciplinary skills than public school. Therefore, he accepted a teaching position in an auto mechanics vocational program at a community college.

In this SIGI PLUS skills assessment subsection, clients choose job titles of interest and answer questions in a skills inventory. They use their self-perceptions to identify skills they already possess. They then relate these skills to the ones needed in other career areas. They are often surprised at the number of skills they already have which will transfer to new career areas. They also become aware of new skills they will have to develop in order to pursue new career directions.

Using the skills assessment in SIGI PLUS, the musician discussed above realized that he had demonstrated more organizational skills in his current profession than he first realized. When comparing his skills to those of business managers and personnel directors, he discovered that he had used many of the skills needed for those jobs throughout his career. For example, he had to use organizational and time management skills when accepting performance requests and arranging travel and lodging.

The results of a skills inventory as well as a review of grades earned in formal training and/or educational programs will be useful in the prediction system of Gelatt's decision-making paradigm.

Values, interests, personality charcteristics and skills are related in that they will directly influence a confused individuals' identification and development of a new life structure, or the acceptance of an existing life structure. I have found that the personality charcteristics, values, interests, and skills each client possesses are not always well integrated.

For example, a young male undergraduate student majoring in accounting came for career counseling. He had excellent grades in accounting (skills), but was bored in most of his classes. He felt no challenge (value) in the course work, although he found the mathematical problem-solving components (personality) of some of his classes mildly interesting (interests) and easy to accomplish (skills). He found the time he spent in his volunteer work as a big brother to be much more satisfying (personality needs and interests) than the time spent in educational pursuits.

When tested with the MBTI, his personality type (ENFP) suggested that he would find more satisfaction in a work environment that allowed him to directly help others using innovative problem-solving skills. The SII indicated a high interest in helping others (Social) through the use of leading and influencing skills (Enterprising). It also indicated an interest in creative problem-solving (Artistic) in which abstract thoughts and ideas took precedence over concrete facts (personality needs).

He had many varied interests some of which were highly compatible with psychologists and other related professions. They were also moderately similar with accountants. His values, as expressed through the Self Assessment and Locate Subsections on the SIGI PLUS system indicated that high income was the highest priority, prestige the second, and business-related interests the third. The skills section of SIGI PLUS reinforced his self perception that he could successfully do accounting functions, and indeed, almost any other skills required by the other occupations he explored.

After exploring several career options, including jobs related to accounting and psychology, this client decided that he would remain in accounting and use his leisure time to satisfy his needs for helping others. His values of prestige, as well as his family's continued pressure to pursue accounting, which was his father's career choice, were more important to the client at this time than any other factor.

He also felt that he could do the work required in accounting and was too close to graduation to change his major. During the decision making process, he predicted that the perceived rewards of staying in his current major outweighed the perceived risks of dissatisfaction with accounting.

One year following graduation, this client returned to my private practice. He was working at a Big Six accounting firm and, although he was very "successful" as evidenced by his performance evaluations and a promotion in the firm, he was very unhappy.

After reprioritizing his values and reviewing his personality characteristics, interests and skills, he decided that income and prestige were not as important as helping others. Even though he could successfully accomplish the tasks in accounting, he found very little satisfaction in his current career. He enjoyed his continued volunteer work in the community. In fact, he was the accounting firm's official representative on several human service agency boards.

After predicting the risks and rewards in accounting with those he perceived he would find in "helping others" careers, he decided he wanted to change his career direction. He, therefore, decided to discuss his concerns with his family. Whether or not he received their approval, he decided to apply to a graduate program in psychology and prepare for a career in counseling.

Career and Educational Information Stage

After identifying, through formal or informal testing, the personality traits, interests, values, and skills of clients, the next phase in the career counseling process is to teach them how to research career and educational information. Using their self-information, the clients screen information about various careers and begin to identify educational needs. Testing may be useful at this stage, especially if the client is considering a training program, whether vocational or academic.

Aptitude and Ability Testing

Cognitive psychology has established a significant amount of research and theory which attempts to describe how individuals learn. There is still much controversy today about the amount of interaction and impact the heredity and social factors have on an individual's: 1) ability to learn, and 2) choice of learning styles.

According to the intelligence theory, aptitude tests predict school performance and success in training better than they do job performance. For this reason, an aptitude test becomes an important assessment tool for clients who are considering entering a formal training program which will require a great commitment of time, energy and money. The aptitude test will support clients decision to either attempt to enter the training, or to seek an alternative career.

Achievement tests are useful for measuring knowledge of most subjects taught in school and diagnosing knowledge deficiencies. If clients are considering returning to formal training, these tests are useful to verify and/or support whether or not they have the necessary abilities, or whether they first need to correct any knowledge deficits before beginning formal training.

In the author's professional experience clients who are considering some formal training are better assessed at a local educational institution or vocational rehabilitation program, than in a counseling practice removed from the actual training program. Once clients have identified a variety of options, specialists in an academic setting can be of significant help in helping the client to determine his/her training potential for given options.

Clients can then also receive accurate up-to-date information on application procedures, program requirements and financial aid information from these or other sources on campus. Once clients have gathered this information, choices can once again be made in the privacy of the career counselor's office.

Job Search Phase

After completing the self assessment and the career and educational planning phases, the client has now identified several career directions. During the job search phase, the career counselor must now help the client to *relearn* effective job search skills. Even if the client decided to enter a formal training program, he or she needs help in learning how to effectively fill out an application, write a resume, and how to "sell" his/herself to others who are evaluating their self-presentation skills.

Use of Computers and Coaching Techniques

During the job search phase, clients may be supervised at a computer as they construct a resume. During this type of session, the counselor coaches clients on how to present themselves to an employer, not only on paper, but in person.

Using roleplay techniques, clients can be encouraged to choose among and then discuss their past work experiences. Using modeling techniques, the counselor can teach methods to present the most appropriate experiences and use professional language to describe these experiences. The client can then be coached in how to present these experiences using the professional language which is most comfortable for them.

Videotape Assessment of Interviewing Skills

After coaching the client on which experiences to highlight for an employer, behavioral techniques like coaching, modeling, shaping and reinforcement can help prepare them for an interview. This could be an interview for a job, or acceptance into a professional school.

Videotaping can ultimately be used to assess clients' current ability to interview effectively. Videotape review can be a very valuable assessment tool. Even those clients who seem to have been successful in past interviewing experiences can benefit from the coaching that occurs when the videotape of a role play is reviewed and critiqued.

Some companies now require that applicants interview on a videotape for later review by a personnel specialist in the company. The career counselor can help to prepare clients for this experience by assessing a videotaped role play and coaching them in more effective interviewing techniques.

Summary

In review, the intake phase is a time for assessing the learning abilities and styles of clients. Learning theory research describes the impact learning styles may have upon career choice. For that reason, clients who may demonstrate difficulties in reading and information comprehension should be referred to a local source to identify any learning deficit(s) and to assess their learning style.

Also during the intake phase a career maturity inventory (Adult Career Concerns Inventory) should be employed to assess the progress and rate clients have made in their career development. This allows one to plan appropriate interventions during later phases.

If the intake interview and career maturity inventory support the need for testing during the self-assessment phase of the counseling process, a trait-factor assessment of the clients' personal characteristics is in order. The personality inventory based upon Jung's theory (Myers-Briggs Type Indicator), an interest inventory based upon John Holland's theory and research (Strong Interest Inventory), a values inventory based upon Martin Katz's theory (SIGI PLUS Self-Assessment Subsection) and a skills inventory, based upon the behavioral reinforcement theory (SIGI PLUS Skills Subsection) are all valuable tools to assess the discrepancies or the similarities in the client's view of self.

Using Gelatt's decision-making paradigm, the self-assessment information is used during the prediction and valuing stages to assess the career information clients gain in informational interviewing, use of written career information and use of the computerized career guidance systems.

During the career and educational information phase, clients who are considering further education or training in order to make a career change can be referred to a local source for an aptitude and/or achievement test(s). This information is used during the predictive stage (based upon knowledge of aptitude and career information) of Gelatt's decision-making model.

During the job search stage, behavioral techniques may be used to reinforce effective interviewing skills and to discourage use of ineffective interviewing skills in critiqued videotape role plays. The tape may be used to model and suggest changes in verbal interchanges and nonverbal behavior which will make for more effective interviewing skills.

Ethical Concerns In Assessment Selection

After considering theoretical orientations and choosing the types of tests to administer to clients, counselors must follow AACD ethical guidelines when selecting actual instruments. Because choice of testing instruments can be legally questioned when used for educational or vocational selection, placement, or counseling the counselor must carefully consider the specific validity, reliability, and appropriateness of the test(s).

Counselors must also recognize their own limitations in competence when interpreting test(s). In other words, they must make sure they have the proper training to understand the meaning of the construct the test is measuring, as well as specific training in the instrument selected for use.

Another ethical concern is related to the use of personal computers in the test administration and scoring process. This issue is addressed in the section below.

Counselors also need to realize that all tests have limitations. For example, while a test can be useful and valid in one situation, it can be completely invalid in another. The counselor must check the validity, reliability and norms before using a test with a particular client. Be critical when evaluating tests for use.

Computerized Career Assessment

One consideration in the selection of specific instruments is how and when to administer them. There are several ways or "hows" available to administer tests. Tests can be administered individually or in groups. They can be hand scored, scored by a computerized testing service, or scored on a personal computer.

In my private practice, I choose to use the personal computer generated test results for the MBTI and the SII. The ACCI is not available at this time on software, but it can be manually scored. Thanks to modern technology, clients may now come into the counseling setting, sit for a test and receive accurate, computer-generated results immediately. This is one of the major reasons that I choose to use computerized testing.

Advantages of Using Computerized Assessment

Immediate scoring capability, the major advantage of using computerized assessment, relieves the test administrator of having to hand score and possibly make mistakes in the scoring.

A second advantage is that it saves postage and the turnaround time it takes to mail out inventories to the companies that score them. Thirdly, it saves the client from having to make a return trip for the results after the administration of the instrument.

A fourth advantage to computerized testing occurs during the test interpretation. It is easier to discuss the instrument with the client and answer questions on the construction or other testing aspects, when the test is still fresh in the client's mind.

Cost Considerations

An important consideration before implementing computerized testing is its cost. I believe it is highly cost effective to incorporate computerized testing into the consulting process. The initial expense for purchasing a computer may seem high until the many functions for which it can be used is considered.

Correspondence and word processing, preparation of handouts, fee schedules and other materials for clients, billing and payments, accounting, testing and preparation of materials, are many of the functions of a private practice.

The first concern of combining client use of the computer with other uses is confidentiality. One must not leave clients alone with the computer. There should always be a staff member available to select the proper assessment instrument or program and monitor its use by the client. Furthermore, when scoring the instrument, the test administrator should ask the client to have a seat in a separate waiting room as the test is scored. The results of the test should not be given to the client until they are escorted to the counselor's office for an immediate test interpretation.

Following is a cost comparison of computerized testing versus manual scoring or sending reports in to computer companies for scoring based on 1990 costs.

Computerized Administration and Scoring

The computer hardware must be IBM PC or compatible and must have at lest 640K memory. Hardware costs vary from $1,000 and up, depending upon current costs in your locale and upon the type of hardware selected. The initial cost of the software system will be approximately $500 and will include; 1) a half size PC board which will have to be installed in your computer, 2) a one year lease to use the software, 3) a user's manual, 4) software for one test (additional software for each test is $50 extra), 5) 10 free test administrations. Additional profile administrations will cost $3 each and additional narrative administrations will cost $5 each.

Therefore it will cost $500 for the initial installation, $300 for 110 administrations and profile reports for the MBTI, $50 to add the SII software, $300 for 110 administrations and profile reports for the SII, for a total cost of $1,150 plus hardware costs. Some companies will lower the cost of the individual administrations and profile reports as the total number of the order increases.

The *ACCI* if self-scored will cost; 1) manual $24, 2) test booklets and profile sheets $7 pack of 25, and 3) answer sheets $20 per package of 50 for hand scoring. The cost runs $6 a test if scored through the test publisher. So, if hand scored, the total cost for the first year to administer 300 ACCI will be $228. If scored by the publisher, 300 administrations will cost $1,800.

The total cost for the year of implementation for 310 administrations and profile scoring of the MBTI and SII on a computer, plus the hand scoring cost of 300 ACCI is $1,378.

Computerized Career Guidance Programs

There are many computerized career guidance programs on the market today. The most important factor to consider when choosing such a system for a private practice is how the system results will be integrated into your counseling process.

For example, the SIGI PLUS system is used to provide a values *clarification* exercise instead of a values ranking exercise. It also includes a skills assessment substage. The results of these exercises are integrated into a self-assessment phase of the counseling process.

Computerized career guidance systems range greatly in price. Some state-sponsored systems cost as little as $75. Other systems cost $2,500 and up. The SIGI PLUS system can be leased for a three year period at a cost of $1,125 per year.

The prices increase as the functions of the system increase. For example, if a system's only function is to provide career information, it will be less expensive than a system which provides self assessment activities, career information and decision-making functions.

Publisher and Hand Scoring

To hand score the *MBTI,* the implementation costs for Form G are; 1) test booklets $12 per package of 25, 2) answer sheets $8.50 per package of 50, 3) scoring keys $15 a set, 4) manual $24, and 5) report forms $6 per package of 50. If hand scored, the annual implementation cost for a minimum of 300 administrations is $151. If scored by the publisher, the prepaid answer sheets cost $65 for a package of 10 for the narrative report and $42 for a package of 10 for the profile report. The total cost for prepaid profile scoring for 300 administrations is $1,260.

The only options for scoring the *SII* are by the publisher or by personal computer. Prices range from $48 per package of 10 ($42 per package of 10 if 100 to 490 are ordered at same time) for the profile report, to $100 per package of 10 for the narrative report. The manual costs $17 and the SII User's Guide costs $15. Therefore, using the profile report costs, the total cost for 300 administrations is $1,440 plus postage for each mailing.

Comparison of Cost

During the first year of implementing a computerized system, it will cost $1,378 (plus hardware costs) for 310 personal computer administrations and scoring of the MBTI and the SII, and 300 hand scored ACCI. It will also cost $1,125 for a year's lease of the SIGI PLUS system, for a total of $2,503. The total cost for 300 hand scored MBTI and ACCI, and 300 publisher scored SII will be $1,819 plus postage.

After the first year, the repeat administrations for the MBTI and the SII are less expensive for the personal computerized testing than for the mail in scoring. For example, the SII administrations are $2.40 each for 100 administrations on the personal computer and $4.80 each if prepaid and mailed in for scoring. The MBTI costs $2.40 each for 100 administrations on the personal computer and $2.85 plus postage each if mailed in for scoring.

71

It is difficult to put a money value on the other functions the computer performs for your private practice. It cuts the time spent in word processing by more than half. It can also cut the time spent in billing clients by almost three fourths. Even if you do these functions yourself, it will save considerable time that can be used for income-generating tasks. If you have secretarial help, it will save you hourly wages, for the tasks can be accomplished more quickly by computer than by hand.

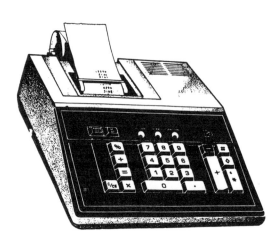

Other cost effective functions the computer can perform are; 1) typing mailing labels rather than individually typing names and address on envelopes, 2) producing handouts rather than paying printing expenses, and 3) maintaining an appointment calendar.

If you are using a computerized career system in the assessment phase of the counseling process, you have the added benefit of having a career library, which is updated yearly, on computer. The client can receive printouts with up-to-date career information to take home with them. The costs of collecting written information for a career library, up-dating that information and reproducing that information for clients is reduced by at least three-fourths.

As with any intervention there are negative as well as positive aspects to computerized testing. The most negative, that of confidentiality, has been addressed. Another negative factor concerns interpretation. The counselor cannot rely solely on computerized interpretations. It is imperative for a counselor to give an individualized interpretation for any test given.

It is also essential for the counselor to demonstrate to the client the interrelationship of the various results and what impact the information gained will have on the client's decision-making process. In other words, the counselor has to teach the client how to use this information in the decision-making process.

A Sample Career Counseling Process

Assessment must be integrated into the total counseling process. Below is described a typical process to use with a client who has been assessed to need all of the following services.

Session One — Needs Assessment and administration of the Adult Career Concerns Inventory with a referral for learning styles/deficiencies testing if necessary.

Session Two — Administration and interpretation of the Myers-Briggs Type Inventory.

Session Three — The administration and interpretation of the Strong Interest Inventory and a discussion on the similarities or discrepancies noted between personality characteristics and interests. Discussion of the learning disabilities/styles assessments, if necessary.

Session Four and Five — Use of the SIGI PLUS Subsections of Self-Assessment and Locate.

Session Six — Discussion of the Values chosen as most important and their interrelationship with personality characteristics and interests. Several career choices are suggested for review in the remaining SIGI PLUS Subsections.

Session Seven and Eight — Use and completion of the SIGI PLUS system (more time allowed as necessary).

Session Nine — Discussion of career choices which are consistent with personality, interests, values and skills. Informational interviewing techniques discussed and questions generated. Referral made to professionals in the client's identified career areas of interest. Discussion, if necessary, about the educational programs available and the application and acceptance process.

Session Ten — If needed, a resume is developed by the counselor and the client at the computer. The resume can be taken on the informational interviews to be critiqued by the career professionals contacted. During the process of writing the resume, the client is coached how to present his or her qualifications and experience using appropriate language for a career change.

Session Ten or Eleven — Discussion of the results of the client's visits with the above named professionals. A plan of action is developed using short term and long term goals. Job search techniques or applications to educational programs discussed as appropriate.

Session Twelve — If appropriate, interviewing techniques for jobs or for professional/graduate school are discussed. A role play of an interview is videotaped and critiqued.

Session Thirteen — Follow up session.

This process is very flexible and can be modified to accommodate clients special needs, such as personal counseling sessions.

In summary, it is important to consider your theoretical orientations and the counseling process you will lead a client through before selecting the assessment instruments you will use in your private practice. The integration of the assessment information with the decision-making process you choose to teach the client is also an important consideration, in the selection and interpretation process you choose. Ethical principles must also be considered. From the assessment instruments you have available select the appropriate ones based upon the intake session results.

Additional Thoughts on "Selecting and Integrating Assessment Into a Private Practice"

Shepard — In response to questions relative to her presentation she added the following information. Thirteen sessions for career counseling are desirable, plus a free follow-up session. The client spends a maximum of 1.5 hours on the computer using SIGI PLUS. A SII video laser interpretation program is used prior to discussion of the SII with the career counselor. See Kapes & Mastie (1988) in the Appendix for additional information on the SII, MBTI, and ACCI.

Herr — He finds Super's *Salience Inventory* helpful in assessing the relative importance of five major life roles for the client. [Editor's Note: See Kapes & Mastie (1988) reference in the Appendix for additional information on the *Salience Inventory*.] The Forer *Vocational Survey: Men-Women* is also useful in assessing personality as related to work situations. [Editor's Note: distributed by Western Psychological Services, Los Angeles.]

Musgrove — She does not use any standardized assessment instruments in her career counseling. She does use an occupational card sort.

Zuber — She uses some testing but is biased against testing.

Hafer — A recent survey of the 287 members of the NCDA Career Counseling in Private Practice Special Interest Group determined that 223 use the SII, 216 the MBTI and 163 the SDS in their career counseling practice. Many large corporations are now using the MBTI in their management training and development programs. It is noted that some of the major outplacement firms and the U.S. Postal Service use the *Personal Profile System* by Performax Systems International, Inc. This assessment instrument is supposed to identify a person's work behavioral style and has 18 different work patterns. I have seen no data relative to the reliability or validity of the *Personal Profile System.*

I use a number of different assessment instruments (A.I.S.) depending upon the career counseling objectives, needs and goals of the client. Some of these are:

Intake — Holland's *My Vocational Situation* (adults) and Osipow's *Career Decision Scale* (adolescents).

Interests — *Career Assessment Inventory* for occupations requiring no more than two years of college. For occupations requiring more than two years of college the *Strong Interest Inventory, Holland's Self-Directed Search* (Forms R and CP) and/or Holland's *Vocational Preference Inventory.* All of these A.I.s are based upon the Holland typologies.

Personality and Traits — *Myers-Briggs Type Indicator,* Jackson's *Personality Research Form (E)* and the *Entrepreneur's Quiz.* [Editor's Note: See Chapter One for a discussion of the latter A.I.]

Career Orientation — Derr's *Career Success Map.* See the Appendix for additional information on this item.

Skills — ACT's *Vocational Interest, Experience & Skill Assessment.*

Career Decision Module — *Kepner-Tregoe Decision Model.* This decision model is used extensively by corporations such as G.E.

Aptitude/Ability Tests — I normally use academic transcript, SAT/ACT socres and work experience for this area. Where an A.I. appears desirable I use the *Differential Aptitude Test.*

Under the section on "Interest Inventories," Dr. Shepard states, "Since one of the basic differences in most interest inventories is the classification system used to report results, there is no need to use more than one interest inventory for each individual client." It is defintely undesirable to use more than one interest inventory if different classification systems are involved. However, several different interest inventories use Holland's typologies, but provide different types of information to the client and counselor. I have used three different interest inventories, all based on the Holland typologies, with assessment instrument.

Strong Interest Inventory — Client scores on the 23 Basic Interest Scales, Extroversion/Introversion scale and Academic Comfort scale are interpreted.

Vocational Preference Inventory (Holland) — In addition to the Holland Code, scores on the following client characteristics are interpreted: self control scale, masculinity scale, status scale, infrequency scale and acquiescence scale.

Self-Directed Search (Holland) — I use form R for clients that are interested in occupations with an educational requirement of two years of college or less, and Form CP for occupations requiring a four year college degree or graduate work. The SDS considers 1,321 occupations whereas the SII considers only 108 occupations and some of these are questionable, e.g. Army, Air Force, and Navy officers and enlisted persons. The SII also lists only one occupation for engineer and yet there are a number of different Holland Codes for different engineering specialties, e.g., mechanical engineer, ceramics engineer, agricultural engineer, computer engineer, aeronautics engineer, etc. The SDS appropriately provides differentiation of these different specialties. It is also easier to explore occupations from the SDS as it lists the U.S. Department of Labor's DOT code. The SII in some cases uses occupational titles that are not included in the 22,000 occupations contained in the *DOT*.

The career counselor starting in private practice is likely to have cash flow problems making it difficult to purchase the necessary computer hardware and software for such systems as SIGI PLUS. I have a very high regard for computer-assisted career guidance systems but at what point can the career counselor economically support such a system? For example, Dr. Shepard based her economic analysis on 300 clients. It will probably take several years to build a private practice to this level. In addition I believe that two personal computers would be required — one for CACG and one for the business end (word processing, data management, mailing labels and accounting). To try and schedule both CACG (with 300 client interventions requiring up to 450 hours/year and secretary/bookkeeper to use the same personal computer presents major scheduling problems. Hopefully computer hardware and software costs will continue to come down so that this will become more feasible in the future. It should be noted that of the 287 NCDA Career Counselors in Private Practice SIG, only 14 say they have a CACG system in their private practice.

Use of assessment instruments in career counseling is one of the distinguishing characteristics of the professional career counselor (another is being a National Certified Career Counselor). Many career consultants and outplacement counselors are not qualified to administer and interpret some of the assessment instruments previously mentioned. I agree with Dr. Shepard that it is important that testing be an integral part of the career counseling process and not as an independent function. Every A.I. used should have a specific and understood purpose, and there should be client agreement relative to the A.I.s used. It is obvious that the more A.I.s used the more time and money must be spent in procurement, administration, scoring and interpretation. In addition, the more A.I.s used the longer the final client written report summarizing the career counseling results.

Dr. Shepard shows a career counseling series involving thirteen sessions at $65 per session, which is $845. I agree that this number of sessions is highly desirable, but my experience is that most clients who must pay for their own sessions will only come four to seven times. An exception is outplacement counseling or spouse relocation where a company is paying for the counseling.

I think Dr. Shepard has provided a comprehensive discussion of a key element in career counseling, i.e., use of assessment instruments and computer-assisted career guidance systems.

Bordin, E.S., Nachmann, B., & Segal, S.J. (1963). An articulated framework for vocational development. *Journal of Counseling Psychology. 10,* 107-116.

Gelatt, H.B. (1961). Decision-making: a conceptual framework for counseling. *Journal of Counseling Psychology. 9*(3), 240-245.

Holland, J.L. (1973). *Making vocational choices: A theory of careers.* Englewood Cliffs, N.J.: Prentice-Hall.

Katz, M. (1973). The name and nature of vocational guidance. In H. Borow (Ed.), *Career guidance for a new age* (p. 83-134). Boston: Houghton Mifflin.

Levitan, S.A. and Johnson, C.M. (1982). The future of work; Does it belong to us or to the robots. *Monthly Labor Review* 105 (9) 60-72.

Lucas, A. (1989) *Encyclopedia of information systems and services.* Detroit: Gale.

McKenny, L.L., & Keen, P.G.W. (1974). How manager's minds work. *Harvard Business Review. 52,* 79-90.

Phifer, P. (1990) *Career planning Q's and A's: A handbook for students, parents, and professionals.* Garrett Park, MD: Garrett Park Press.

Powell, C.R. (1990) *Career planning today: Second edition: Hire me.* Dubuque: Kendall/Hunt.

Super, D.E., Starishesky, R., Matlin, N., & Jordaan, J.P. (1963). *Career development: Self concept theory.* New York: College Entrance Examination Board.

Chapter Six — Professional Private Practice Marketing Considerations

Michael Shahnasarian
Career Consultants of America
Tampa, FL

This chapter describes a marketing plan which I initially developed for Career Consultants of America, Inc., along with subsequent marketing activities implemented once the practice was established. I define marketing as what you do to get the phone to ring; that is, the activities used to generate interest among prospective clients. Selling, on the other hand, is what you do after the phone rings in order to convert the inquirer to a client. My hope is that this chapter will stimulate some ideas to help you market and grow in your private practice.

Most career counselors admit to having little or no training in the business aspects of a private practice. Perhaps the most important of these areas is the marketing of your services. As we all know, although we may possess excellent counseling skills, be expert on the local and national labor markets, and offer outstanding resources for helping clients in their career decision making and planning, without clients we have no practice.

The fundamental marketing questions all career counselors must ultimately address are deceptively simple. Perhaps it is this simplicity that lulls so many to leap into their practices before developing a sound marketing plan. Three critical questions that should underlie your marketing plan follow.

1. Why are you in business? What is your motivation, aim,

and mission in going into private practice? Your answer should attempt to address the following: client base you plan to cultivate; volume of clients for different services; type of career guidance services you plan to offer; and, sales goals you aspire to attain.

2. Why should clients come to you for services? That is, what is the value-added you offer over other practitioners from which prospective clients may choose?

3. When clients seek your services, what do they get? I recommend that you write out your response to this question and share it with a few individuals who you can count on for a candid response.

Most successful career counselors agree that marketing is a vital, ongoing part of their business plans. The notion that once a practice is established, counselors can relax their efforts, and the momentum the practice gains will suffice, is largely a myth. I use the word "largely" because there are rare occasions and circumstances in which this may happen, but my experience has been that this is certainly the exception rather than the rule.

Since marketing is so vital to your practice's success it pays to invest in developing these skills. Attending seminars, interacting with marketing and sales professionals from other service industries, and studying the myriad of self-directed resources available will help to refine your skills and comfort level. These activities will stimulate your thinking about marketing techniques applicable to your own practice and, perhaps most important, keep you motivated to continue an activity in which you likely received little professional training and in which your comfort level may be low.

The following describes the marketing plan I developed for my practice, Career Consultants of America (CCA) in Tampa, Florida. The success of services CCA offered to the public, namely the "Planning Your Career Program" for youth, career counseling, and vocational testing, depended largely upon the success of its marketing campaign — this was especially the case during the practice's first year. Since the majority of CCA's revenues were expected to be generated through services rendered to community-based clients in CCA's office, the image CCA projected to the community was of prime concern.

Professional Image

CCA's services have two different markets 1) members of the Tampa Bay community, and 2) business organizations throughout the United States. To members of the Tampa Bay community, CCA offers the following services: career counseling, vocational testing, job campaign services, and special programs for youth. To business organizations, CCA offers consulting services on establishing internal career development programs, spouse relocation services, and training in various management and career development topics.

Consumers of CCA services are by and large, relatively affluent, well-educated individuals. That is, the majority of its clients are college-educated, have been in the workforce a minimum of three years, and have an earning's history of at least $35,000 per year. Since CCA aspires to provide the highest quality of career development services available in the Tampa Bay area and since its services are priced accordingly, CCA's image had to reflect its professional, high quality orientation. This image has been maintained through the following:
- Delivery of superior quality personal services.
- Services provided by a qualified professional(s).
- Support staff who are well trained, courteous and who project a professional image.
- Responsible, ethical practice.
- An office located in a professional office complex. The office is furnished in conservative good taste.
- High quality, professional-looking materials.
- A professional, but aggressive, advertising and marketing campaign.
- Pricing comparable to or above other providers of career development services in the Tampa Bay area.

Pricing

Consistent with its strategy to project CCA as a provider of superior quality career development services, CCA's services were priced at or above its competitions'. A price schedule was developed for four different types of services as follows:

Career Counseling (individual clients) — price per hour.

"Planning Your Career Program" — price per participant.

Vocational Testing — price per participant for either (a) comprehensive assessment, or (b) an abbreviated assessment.

Corporate Consulting — price per hour, with a retainer schedule available for extended engagements.

Market Analysis

The Tampa Bay area was experiencing an economic expansion in 1987, the year I committed to my practice full-time. To make sound business decisions on targeting potential clients and allocating marketing efforts and resources, a comprehensive market analysis was in order. To this end, I consulted numerous research sources to investigate a myriad of marketing decisions ranging from site selection to the design of promotional brochures. Summarized below is information found to be most relevant in developing the marketing plans.

Statistical analysis of the Tampa Bay area's growth revealed the following:

- —Population in Hillsborough County rose 17.2% from 1981 to 1986.
- —The Tampa Bay region accounted for nearly a fifth of the new vehicle registrations from states outside of Florida.
- —Housing starts rose 84% in Hillsborough County in 1986 compared with 1981

Hillsborough County's 1986 population was estimated at 775,000 by *Florida Trend;* the projected population in 1991 is 886,000. According to a Louis Harris survey reported in the July 7, 1987 *Tampa Tribune,* the number of families in Tampa with annual pretax income of $75,000 or more would increase 143% in the next five years. The survey also reported that 37,136 Tampa households already had such incomes, and it was projected that the number would increase to 90,330 by 1991.

It appeared that the demographic characteristics of Tampa, in general, and CCA's location, in particular, were favorable to CCA's proposed site and plans for business development. In addition to consulting relevant quantitative data, I informally surveyed several hundred parents of teenage children on their opinions of the "Planning Your Career Program", a career guidance program I developed for youth and projected would account for over 50% of CCA's revenues. While this is, of course, an imprecise method for gauging prospective client demands, my survey found overwhelming support for the program.

Analysis of Competition

My analysis of colleagues already in private practice consisted of the following:

An examination of practitioners who advertised in the Tampa yellow pages.

Telephone calls to each practitioner. During these calls I asked about the services provided, fees, and available literature or descriptive information.

A review of literature describing available career guidance services.

Telephone calls to 30 randomly selected psychologists and counselors. I conducted these calls to determine if these practitioners had established referral relationships with local career counselors.

The 1987 Tampa yellow pages listed five practitioners under the category "Career Counseling" and 11 practitioners under the category "Vocational." Two practitioners were listed under both categories. Of the five service providers listed under "Career Counseling," three were in business at the time of the call. Of the 11 practitioners listed under "Vocational," only three provided career guidance services. The others provided vocational rehabilitation services. Other than yellow page listings, I was unaware of other advertisements of career development services or other practitioners in the Tampa Bay area.

The following was a summary I compiled on my eventual colleagues in private practice.

Career Counseling Practice B — The testing fee included an initial consultation to determine the instruments that would be given to the client and an interpretation session. They had a licensed psychologist on their staff. Typical areas of career counseling included employability skills development and helping clients become employed. The person I spoke with indicated that this was a relatively new business. She said they had no special programs and no brochures. She indicated that they were concerned with survival at first, and now they are busy trying to keep up with the business they currently had.

Career Counselor C — He selected an assessment battery for each client. Tests he typically used included: Mini Minnesota Multiphasic Personality Inventory, 16 PF, and the Kuder Occupational Interest Survey. The interpretation session was conducted at an extra fee. He was a clinical psychologist, and he estimated that only 20 to 25 percent of his time was spent on career development work. He mentioned that he had a computerized assessment system in his office, clients took the tests on line.

Career Counselor D — The yellow page listing announced the following: Job search and career change program, and testing. He charged an hourly rate for testing rather than a fee for the battery. He said he specialized in mid-life career change for adults. The testing he administered typically included interests, abilities, and personality. The average number of sessions required to complete the testing ranged between three and five one-hour sessions. He said he prescribed homework and library assignments to his clients between sessions.

Career Counselor E — In addition to providing individual career guidance services, he indicated that he also provided consulting services to corporations. His assessment process involved three sessions: 1) initial interview, 2) testing (usually lasted 6 - 8 hours), and 3) debriefing session.

Career Counselor F — He had variable testing rates, depending on the clients' career experience. His assessment included: intelligence, values, aptitude, and interests. After he interpreted the tests he wrote a report and presented it to the client during the debriefing. He also had a career library available for his clients' use. He sent me a form letter outlining his testing process. His letterhead listed him along with seven other consulting psychologists with offices in Tampa and Jacksonville. The Tampa office is located in the "X" Center, a large office building with no visibility from the street.

Career Counselor G — Testing process involved an interview, test administration, and interpretive session. She also leads personal growth groups and specialized in therapy. Her office is closed on Fridays.

Career Counseling Firm H — This practice reported that they administered a battery of tests on a range of aptitudes, including dexterity and music. Testing lasted 1½ days. Interpretation of the test result was priced separately and the practice does not provide career counseling services other than test interpretation. They sent me a brochure and several article reprints referencing their organization. They are located in the "Y" Center, a large office building with no visibility from the street.

As indicated above, only two practitioners provided literature to their prospective clients. From my survey of area psychologists and counselors I also learned that three of the practitioners identified above most often received referrals. Perhaps as many as 50% of the psychologists and counselors I surveyed were unaware of a career development professional who would be an appropriate referral source.

It appeared that my eventual colleagues in private practice were primarily offering testing and counseling services. I did not identify another practitioner in the Tampa Bay area who offered a program for youth similar to CCA's "Planning Your Career" program.

Value-Added Features of
Career Consultants of America

After my analysis of colleagues in established private practices, my task was to determine the value-added features that would likely attract prospective clients to CCA. That is, why would an individual in need of career guidance services choose CCA over another practice? I determined CCA's value-added features to include the following:

- Services provided by an experienced career guidance professional with a doctorate in counseling psychology, and who was a National Certified Career Counselor (NCCC).

- While most of my colleagues also held a doctorate degree, I was unaware of another practitioner in the Tampa Bay area who was a National Certified Career Counselor. As in any service business, it is the expertise and credential of the practicing professional that is of value to the consumer.

- Holistic, full-service development services which included vocational assessment, career counseling, career information resources, job campaign services, and special programming for youth.

- High quality, proven career guidance resources (e.g., validated vocational assessment instruments, computer-based guidance programs, availability of reference materials, etc.).

- An accessible location to clients most lkely (in terms of demographic characteristics) to patronize CCA.

One initial limitation of CCA was a modest library of career resources available to its clients, e.g., descriptive information about occupations, wage and salary information, labor market projections for various occupations, etc. This was not a major disadvantage, however, as I was aware of only one practitioner in the area who maintained a career resources library. As CCA became profitable, funds were budgeted for the library and the library ultimately grew to become another value-added feature of CCA.

Marketing Vehicles

Eight different marketing vehicles CCA used to promote business during its first year are described below.

Presentations to professional and community groups — I developed a professional slide show (the cost of this production was approximately $1,000) to describe the "Planning Your Career Program" to potential clients. I presented this slide show to many community and professional groups in the Tampa Bay area including PTA groups in high schools, local community service organizations (e.g., Rotary Clubs, Kiwanis Clubs, Lions Clubs, etc.) and continuing education seminars for school counselors and occupational specialists. At the end of these presentations I distributed a brochure on the "Planning Your Career Program."

Planning Your Career brochure — 2,000 copies of a four color, 4" x 8½" brochure that described the "Planning Your Career Program" were produced. I distributed these brochures at: a) presentations I made, b) to individuals cultivated as a referral network, and c) to clients who inquired about the program.

Referral network — Through personal visitations and a letter campaign, CCA established relationships with a network of allied professionals who later became excellent referral sources. Among these professionals were psychologists and counselors in private practice, school counselors, and administrators at a local organization that provided instruction in preparing for a variety of admissions tests, e.g., SAT, GRE, GMAT and other tests required for admission to a professional school.

CCA quarterly newsletter, Career Directions — CCA published a quarterly newsletter entitled *Career Directions* (refer to sample shown in Figure 6-1). Each issue is one page printed on both sides and featured a lead article on a general career-related topic, e.g., managing a dual career relationship, moving beyond the entry level job, making career decisions, etc. An "In the Spotlight" column presented a CCA service or featured a counselor on our staff. Also a description of CCA services and the type of individuals who are appropriate candidates for these services. I purchased a mailing list of 2,000 individuals in the proximity of my office who met requisite demographic characteristics and distributed *Career Directions* to these individuals.

Yellow pages advertising — CCA listed a display ad in the local telephone yellow pages.

General newspaper advertising — CCA advertised on Sundays and on weekdays in the classified section of the local newspaper and in a local business publication.

Articles on career development in local publications — An ongoing component of my marketing plan was to write guest articles on various career development topics for publication in local print media.

Guest appearances as a Tampa Bay area labor market expert on local news and television talk shows — Volunteering to discuss various career development topics proved to have human interest value to the local media and offered excellent visibility to myself and CCA, which helped generate numerous client inquiries.

Marketing Budget: First Year

Tracking data was kept on the sources of client referrals and return on investment ratios were computed to determine the cost effectiveness of CCA's respective marketing vehicles. The marketing budget for the first year was broken into the following categories:

Yellow Pages
Signage
Mailing Lists
Newsletter
     a) Layout
     b) Printing
     c) Postage
Brochures
     a) Artwork
     b) Printing
Newspaper Advertising
     a) Tampa Tribune — Sundays (Full run)
     b) Tampa Tribune by Zone (Partial run)

As a general rule of thumb, it is recommended that you allocate approximately 6 to 8 percent of your practice's projected gross revenues in the first year to marketing activities.

Analysis of costs

1. The newsletter was sent to 2,000 homes each quarter in the first year. Bulk mail rates were 12.5 cents per piece at that time.

2. A one-inch advertisement that included color (red) and the CCA logo was placed in the Tampa Bay yellow pages. The cost on an

Figure 6-1   CCA's Quarterly Newsletter

Volume 2, Number 1   Spring 1989

Career Directions

A Quarterly Newsletter of Career Consultants of America, Inc.

Money As The First Career Priority

by Michael Shahnasarian, Ph.D.

One day a young client said to me: "I'm thinking of going into advertising, but in that field I would be making only $70,000 a year." Reflecting on my knowledge of the local compensation rates, I said to the client, "Let me correct your grammar; I don't believe that ONLY and $70,000 go very well together in the same sentence."

It is easy for us to make light of it, but financial security is no longer a laughing matter to today's college graduate. Loaded with debt and fearful of the financial struggles that lie ahead (some may not have been deprived as children, but they have *heard* it can happen), they "can't afford" to fool around while others are grabbing up the good jobs.

One might think that today's graduates have no concern about anything in their career choices except money. On the contrary, other motives beat in the heart of most young people, but they are often beneath the drive to survive. Truly discovering one's values,

> ## A Message To Our Clients...
>
> We appreciate your past, present and future interest in our professional services and we welcome the opportunity to be of continued service. Please keep us in mind as you identify your career development needs in 1989.

interests and talents is sometimes postponed two to three or more years while the young person gets established and builds a base of experience and a financial backlog. They seem to be more willing to reflect and act upon their long-term goals once they know the system will not swallow them up.

The economics of being a new college graduate have made some graduates delay the time when they can make career commitments. But I believe they still want to reach this deeper level of decision making — after they are certain they can survive in our competitive society.

Because of his expertise on the Tampa Bay labor market, Dr. Michael Shahnasarian, Executive Director of Career Consultants of America, is a frequent guest on local television programs. Here he is shown in a recent appearance with Jack Harris on Pulse Plus.

IN THE SPOTLIGHT

Two New Services To Promote Your Job Campaign

Career Trends

Career Consultants of America has assisted clients with their job campaigns in the past by offering resume writing services, information on employers, help in developing polished interviewing skills, and counseling to discuss issues unique to the client. It now offers two new services to promote its clients' job campaigns.

The first service is a four-hour workshop, *Conducting the Successful Job Campaign*. This practical and dynamic workshop gives many valuable tips to help you get the job you want. Identifying employers who have a need for your talents, making a winning presentation, and negotiating for the best salary and compensation package are among the many topics covered.

Participants' reactions to the workshop have included the following: "I can't tell you enough how much I value this workshop — it has helped me, my husband and son (I know this because the resources will be used by all three)". . . "Gave me excellent guidelines to reach my career goals" . . . and, "Well presented and professional."

The second service is a job club that meets once a week for one and one-half hours. The job club involves working meetings in which members share job leads, discuss problems and questions in their job campaigns, and offer support and encouragement.

Michael Shahnasarian, Ph.D., conducts the workshop and supervises the job club. He has provided career counseling services to over two thousand individuals.

For more information on the job club or the *Conducting the Successful Job Campaign* workshop call (813) 264-2224.

Career Consultants of America's Services

Career Consultants of America is a career counseling practice dedicated to enhancing its clients' career development. To this end, it helps clients make career decisions, plan how they will realize short and long term goals, and conduct successful job campaigns. For more information on the services listed below call (813) 264-2224.
- Career Counseling
- Vocational Testing
- Job Campaign Assistance

Career Directions is published by Career Consultants of America, Inc., 10919 N. Dale Mabry, Tampa, FL 33618, (813) 264-2224.

Career Consultants of America, Inc.
10919 N. Dale Mabry
Tampa, FL 33618

(Note: Since this newsletter was written the phone number was changed to 813/933-4088.)

ad meeting these specifications was approximately $120/month.

3. Four mailings of CCA's newsletter were made during the practice's first year. Each mailing targeted to 2,000 homes, and cost approximately $1,000.

4. Sign costs were for attractive signage outside CCA's office that was visible to passing motorists.

5. Printing costs for the newsletter were based on the assumptions that: a) four issues would be published during the first year (one issue each quarter), b) 2,000 copies of each issue would be printed, and c) the newsletters would be printed on 8½ x 11" heavy stock, colored paper.

6. Prices for mailing lists were quoted by a local marketing company according to the following rates; a) the cost per 1,000 addresses with names was $30, b) targeted marketing options cost $4 each (e.g., renter/homeowner, ages of children, income level, etc.), and c) peel-off labels, cost $10 per 1,000 labels.

7. The labor required to execute the newsletter layout was subcontracted for $50 per issue.

8. Advertising costs in the local newspaper were based on the following rates; a) Full run rate (entire distribution) — $47/column inch, b) Partial run rate when the advertisement was restricted to designated zone(s) — $13/column inch.

These advertising rates were applied to the following assumptions about CCA's advertising strategy to compute annual newspaper advertising costs:

—CCA purchased full runs of four column inch advertisements in five Sunday editions of the local newspaper during its first year (total cost = $940). Sunday advertisements were scheduled as follows:

> January 1988 .... 2 advertisements
> February 1988 .... 1 advertisement
> May 1988 .... 1 advertisement
> September 1988 .... 1 advertisement

CCA also purchased partial runs of four column inch advertisements in 16 weekly editions of the local newspaper during its first year (total cost = $830). These advertisements appeared in the following months:

January	1 advertisement
February	1 advertisement
March	2 advertisements
April	2 advertisements
May	1 advertisement
June	2 advertisements
July	2 advertisements
August	1 advertisement
September	1 advertisement
October	1 advertisement
November	1 advertisement
December	1 advertisement

Scheduled Marketing Activities: First Year

CCA's marketing strategy was under continuous review, including detailed monthly, quarterly and annual analyses of progress on production goals and analyses of the effectiveness of various marketing vehicles in generating business.

Presentations on the "Planning Your Career Program" to various community groups and organizations were an important, ongoing marketing activity. These presentations lasted approximately 20 to 30 minutes and were structured around the slide show developed to

describe the program. Brochures were also distributed during each presentation.

Marketing activities planned for the first year are outlined below. This schedule of activities was adjusted as information on the effectiveness of various marketing strategies was evaluated. An article describing CCA's practice was prominently featured as the lead article in a Sunday edition of the local newspaper during the second quarter of CCA's operation.

Summary of Marketing Activities:

First Year of Operation

— January (one time) — letter to area counselors announcing new practice; occupied office, installed signage, and placed two ads in Sunday edition of the local newspaper.
— Issued quarterly the newsletter: January, April, July, October.

- —Conducted presentations to service clubs, etc. on the "Planning Your Career Program." Goal was two presentations per month.
- —Local newspaper ads — Three months have one ad in a Sunday edition, four months have two ads in weekday partial run edition, and four months have two ads in weekday partial edition.
- —Monthly, reviewed progress on production goals and tracked referrals by marketing vehicles.
- —Yellow pages — submitted information by June (cutoff date). New phone book out in September.
- —Continuously approach media with ideas for featuring various career development topics.

Note: Yellow page cutoff date varies in different parts of the country.

Scope and Description of CCA's Services

Today CCA offers a diversity of services which include career counseling, vocational testing, career development seminars, outplacement, spouse relocation, management training and consulting, and organizational career development. A brief description of each of these services follows.

Career Counseling and Vocational Testing — The sales model used for describing these services and generating interest in prospective clients is shown in Figure 6-2. As can be seen from this figure the sales model should be specific, succinct, comprehensive, professional, and facilitate *getting the client's commitment*. Prices for the services are included in the sales plan. A brochure used to describe these services to clients is shown. A schedule of the six recommended sessions for CCA's vocational testing program is shown in Figure 6-3.

Career Development Seminars — Figure 6-3 also describes two career development seminars offered by CCA. Figure 6-4 presents a typical promotional flyer for a CCA seminar. Topics covered, qualifications of the presenter and registration details including seminar price are among the details presented to prospective seminar attendees.

Management Training Services — One major component of CCA's service line included management training services offered to business organizations. In promoting these services in sales presentations and in advertising literature, CCA's value-added was noted by emphasizing the following:
- • CCA has trained over 5,000 professionals on more than 30

92

Figure 6-2   Sales Model

I.   Begin by first briefly learning the client's needs
    A.   Prior education
    B.   Prior work experience
    C.   Situational factors (e.g., currently working, etc.)
    D.   Career Issues

II.   Describe CCA testing program
    A.   Five meetings: Describe each phase in some detail
        1.   Indicate that program helps to eliminate trial and error career decisions making.
        2.   During description of the process, relate the program back to client's situation whenever possible.
    B.   Address client questions
        1.   Cost
            a.   Summarize that entire program involves approximately four to four and a half hours of career counseling, seven to eight hours of testing, all administration and scoring costs, and the cost of all materials including instruments and workbook . . . the fee is $475.00.
            b.   Note the 3 payments options.
            c.   Handle potential objections — put cost in relative terms (e.g., a car repair)
            d.   If the fee is absolutely beyond client's budget, recommend starting with hourly counseling.
        2.   How long does it take?
            a.   Usually three to five weeks
            b.   The process can be accelerated if necessary.
            c.   The most important thing is to schedule the first meeting so testing can commence.
        3.   What is CCA's background?
            a.   CCA has been in business four years.
            b.   Credentials of the career counselor
            c.   Discuss past client types.
    C.   Advance the sale *(very important step)*
            a.   Ask — when can you start?
            b.   Note we typically require scheduled sessions.
            c.   Recommend two times consistent with counselor's schedule.

III.   Summarize
    A.   Confirm that the client has made a good decision assuming the client needs career counseling.
    B.   Encourage client to bring materials that might be helpful (e.g., resumes, job descriptions, portfolios, transcripts, etc.)

Figure 6-3   Career Guidance Services

Career Guidance Services

Career Consultants of America helps clients with a range of career issues through three types of services: career counseling, vocational testing, and career development seminars.

Career Counseling

Clients with special career needs benefit most from professional career counseling. Career counseling sessions typically focus on: career decision making, career planning, job campaign assistance, resume writing, fine-tuning interviewing skills, negotiating job offers, and long-term career development.

Career Guidance Services

Vocational Testing Program

Career Consultants of America's *Vocational Testing Program* is the most popular service it offers. This comprehensive program, in greatest demand among career changers, young adults, and people re-entering the world of work, includes six phases.

Phase I: Intake Session

Phase II: Testing — Personality, Values and Interests

Phase III: Testing — Aptitudes

Phase IV: Interpretation of Test Results and Recommendations

Phase V: Counseling on Career Decision Making and Planning

Phase VI: Progress Review (one quarter after Phase V)

Career Development Seminars

Conducting The Successful Job Campaign — A must for anyone planning to enter the labor market. This one-half day workshop provides valuable insight and tips on getting ready for the labor market, conducting the job campaign, and negotiating the job offer and focusing on long-term career objectives.

Planning Your Career — Designed for young adults, this program is conducted over a four to six-week period and includes vocational testing, career counseling, and two small group meetings in which participants learn about available options in the world of work and discuss topics like taking SATs, applying to colleges, and selecting a major. The *Planning Your Career Program* received national attention in a 1987 publication of human resource development professionals.

94

Figure 6-4   Conducting the Successful Job Campaign

CONDUCTING THE
SUCCESSFUL JOB CAMPAIGN

a one-half day workshop on strategies for success in your job search

TOPICS

- Writing the Right Resume
- Finding and Converting Leads to Offers
- Making a Winning Presentation
- Negotiating the Best Offer

PRESENTER

Michael Shahnasarian, Ph. D., will conduct the workshop. The President of Career Consultants of America, Inc., Dr. Shahnasarian is a certified career counselor and a licensed mental health counselor. He has provided career counseling services to over 2,000 individuals. Dr. Shahnasarian has appeared in numerous television and radio interviews to share his expertise on the Tampa Bay labor market.

REGISTRATION

Conducting the Successful Job Campaign will be conducted from 9:00 a.m. to 1:00 p.m. on Saturday, February 16, 1991. Reservations are required.
Program fee is $85.00

Career Consultants
of America, Inc.
933-4088

different topics in organizations throughout North America.

- CCA is experienced in the design and conduct of custom management training.
- CCA's corporate clients have included very reputable organizations including Fortune 500 organizations, Big Six accounting firms, and Federal Government organizations.
- CCA's counselors have held leadership positions in a local professional organization consisting of training professionals.
- Industries CCA has specialized in include, accounting, professional associations, telecommunications, government, and banking.
- CCA offers the full range of training and development services, including: 1) needs assessment, 2) curriculum design, 3) instructional design, 4) program development, 5) training, 6) train-the-trainer, and 7) evaluation.

Figure 6-5 displays a general flyer sent to prospective corporate clients. Figure 6-6 presents a flyer which describes various management training courses offered by CCA. Another mailout piece designed to capture potential clients' attention by including a simple test to determine the organization's training and development needs is displayed in Figure 6-7. The bottom of this mailout piece includes a tear-off section making it easy for the prospective client organization to obtain additional information.

Spouse Relocation and Outplacement Service — Two other services CCA offers to corporate clients are career counseling services for relocated spouses and outplacement services. The sales features CCA promotes to generate sales of these two services follows:

- Our value-added services, rendered by Ph.D.s highly experienced in career counseling thousands of clients and are recognized nationally in state-of-the-art career guidance applications like computer-based career guidance, provide a full range of career guidance services local and national in scope.
- Average length of time between when services are rendered and when the person is employed has been 2.8 months. This is 100% of clients employed . . . and is well beyond: a) head hunters' rate, b) typical projections of career counselors, and c) better than industry average.
- CCA is considered expert on the local labor market as evidenced by: a) frequent television appearances to address a number of career areas, b) articles written in a number of local and national publications, c) presentations made at a number of community organizations and national meetings of professional organizations, and d) leadership in national and community organizations.

Figure 6-5 Career Consultants of America . . . An Important Mission

Career Consultants of America

Whether your organization's strategic plan calls for maintaining its position in the marketplace, for expanding gradually, or for aggressively charging ahead of your competition, success will depend largely on how well prepared your employees are to assume tomorrow's challenges. Career Consultants of America, Inc., helps organizations gain the competitive edge.

CCA is a national organization that specializes in career consulting and management consulting services. Headquartered in Tampa, Florida, its consultants are strategically located throughout the United States and are also available to provide services at client locations.

Career Consultants of America... An Important Mission

Among CCA's clients are a number of leading international organizations, including banks, brokerage firms, and big eight accounting firms. Its clients also include organizations in the health care, communications, manufacturing, and high tech industries, as well as national professional organizations.

CCA provides professional services facilitated by individuals with the highest level of expertise, and credentials. Professionalism, conservatism and the maintenance of clients' best interests hallmark CCA's values. Thus, unity, communication and the subordination of self-gain on behalf of its clients is fundamental to CCA's management philosophy, and is a spirit that characterizes the entire staff.

Profile of the President

Michael Shahnasarian, Ph.D., is the president and founder of Career Consultants of America, Inc. One of the first professionals recognized as a nationally certified career counselor in the United States, Dr. Shahnasarian is also a licensed professional counselor and a member of the American Psychological Association. A polished, dynamic speaker who presents programs to thousands of individuals annually, Dr. Shahnasarian is a nationally recognized authority on career development and management development.

Dr. Shahnasarian's credentials include a doctorate in counseling psychology and human systems from Florida State University, a master's degree in psychology from Texas A&M University, and a bachelor's degree in psychology from Indiana University. While completing his doctorate he participated in some well-publicized research on computer assisted career guidance funded by the W.K. Kellogg Foundation.

His publication record includes over a dozen articles on career development practice in industry and academic publications, and a popular career planning workbook entitled *Making Career Decisions*.

Because of his expertise on career development, Dr. Shahnasarian is frequently consulted in television interviews on topics associated with the labor market and issues pertinent to career changers. He has made numerous presentations at national conventions and has participated in an international teleconference on technology in career development.

Dr. Shahnasarian has held leadership positions in a number of national professional associations and local community service organizations. In 1990 Dr. Shahnasarian will assume the presidency of the Suncoast Chapter of the American Society of Training and Development, a 500 member organization of training professionals in the Tampa Bay area. Price Waterhouse presented Dr. Shahnasarian with an award for his business leadership in 1988.

Michael Shahnasarian, Ph.D.

Figure 6-6   Management Training Services

Management Training Services

Management Training Services

Career Consultants of America, Inc., trains thousands of managers each year in the successful practice of leadership and motivation, supervision, sales management, and career counseling. Through skilled instructional design and dynamic classroom instruction, Career Consultants of America offers customized training that focuses on transferring learning to the workplace.

Its well-rounded curriculum of management development courses allows Career Consultants of America to help organizations develop employee potential.

Overview of Courses

Career Coaching and Mentoring (One day) — Designed for managers with staff supervisory responsibilities, this course addresses the career development process and presents techniques for developing talented personnel in line with organizational goals.

Developing Your Career (Three one-half day sessions) — To help staff develop long term careers within their organization and to help them attain balance in their lives, the program includes psychological and vocational assessment, discussion on career development strategies, and individual career counseling.

Effective Communications (Two days) — Beginning with an overview of the communication process, this course focuses on areas vital to successful organizational communication: business writing, conducting successful meetings, and delivering effective presentations.

Negotiations (One day) — An intensive program on determining negotiating ranges, identifying negotiables, and applying negotiating strategies.

Presentation Excellence (Two days) — Participants receive instruction, engage in videotaped presentations, and receive individual coaching on delivering polished, professional presentations.

Supervisor Survival (One day) — For the new supervisor or manager, this course outlines the keys to successful supervision, including: time management, effective delegation, conducting effective meetings, project management, strategic planning, and maintaining positive working relationships.

Team Building, Leadership and Motivation (One day) — Participants learn to identify motivational problems, apply effective motivational techniques, and determine appropriate leadership styles to improve team performance.

The Champion Sales Manager (Two days) — An advanced program on developing marketing plans, business development strategies, and sales management techniques.

Train-The-Trainer (Two days) — A comprehensive course on the art of effective instruction. The course includes discussion on techniques for designing and delivering instruction, and provides opportunities for videotaped practice teaching with individual coaching.

Other Training Services

☐ Curriculum Design
☐ Needs Assessment
☐ Program Development and Evaluation
☐ Organizational Training Plans

Figure 6-7   Employee Peformance

EMPLOYEE PERFORMANCE

▼ **Meeting Organizational Goals.** ▼
Do Your Employee's Have The Right Stuff?

Whether your organization's strategic plan calls for maintaining its position in the marketplace, for expanding gradually, or for aggressively charging ahead of your competition, success will depend largely on how well prepared your employees are for tomorrow. Take the quiz below to help you determine your employees' training and career development needs.

T F My employees' productivity meets my expectations.

T F For the most part, my employees are well-equipped to assume the positions immediately above them.

T F My employees' performance is as good as or better than their counterparts' performance in competitor organizations.

T F The managers in my organization are effective leaders, mentors and role models for employees.

T F My organization uses its employees to their best potential and has plans to develop them in line with short term and long term goals.

T F In examining my employees, I am confident that they possess the talent necessary to keep my organization competitive.

T F I consider my employees' an asset to my own career development.

0 - 1 False: Keep up the good work! Your organization obviously realizes the value of developing its employees.

2 - 3 False: Examine the areas in which your organization needs to improve and plan now for your employees' development.

4 - 7 False: Consider this a warning! If your organization is to reach its potential, retain talented employees, avoid costly attrition, and keep competitive it needs to attend to employee training and career development.

Detach and mail promptly so that we can help you maximize ▼ your employees' performance.

Career Consultants of America, Inc., provides training and career development services to corporations throughout North America. Please complete the information below and indicate which services you would like further information on.

Name _____   Title _____

Organization _____   Telephone Number _____

Address _____

Check the services you are interested in offered by

Career Consultants of America
10919 North Dale Mabry, Tampa, Florida 33618
813-264-2224

CAREER DEVELOPMENT SERVICES

☐ Succession Planning
☐ Spouse Relocation Counseling
☐ Selection Testing

TRAINING AREAS

☐ Mentoring and Career Coaching
☐ Sales Training
☐ Management Training

CONSULTATION IN TRAINING AND DEVELOPMENT

☐ Needs Assessment   ☐ Program Development
☐ Training Plans   ☐ Evaluation

99

Figure 6-8   Spouse Career Counseling Services

Spouse Career Counseling Services

The dual career couple and the increasing rate of employee relocations have become commonplace among American corporations. Together, these trends have encouraged more corporations to offer career guidance services to the trailing spouse in an employee relocation.

Spouse Career Counseling Services

Spouse career counseling services have proven to be cost effective, and have helped organizations conduct more successful relocations, reduce transfer denial rates, and, perhaps most important, have helped organizations to develop and — in many cases — to retain talented employees who are reluctant to forsake their spouses' career development.

Career Consultants of America has long been recognized as a leader in spouse career counseling services. Its services accommodate the diverse needs of trailing spouses. CCA also offers a one day training program on the psychological issues associated with relocation; this program is designed for an organization's employees who are involved in the relocation process. These services are outlined below.

Spouse Career Counseling Services
The career guidance needs of trailing spouses are diverse. Those considering a career change, for instance, benefit from assessment and professional career counseling that aids in career decision making and career planning. Trailing spouses who have already committed to a career path, on the other hand, benefit most from assistance in conducting a successful job campaign.

Career Consultants of America offers three service options to meet trailing spouses' needs.

Option I
Pre-move Counseling and Research
Vocational Testing: Values, Interests, and Skills
Private Career Counseling: 6 hours
Cover Letter and Resume Preparation
Seminar on Conducting a Successful Job Campaign
Circulation and Coordination of Interviews
Monthly Progress Reports to the Organization

Option II
Pre-move Counseling and Research
Vocational Testing: Values, Interests, and Skills
Private Career Counseling: 4 hours
Seminar on Conducting a Successful Job Campaign
Monthly Progress Reports to the Organization

Option III
Pre-move Counseling and Research
Private Career Counseling: 2 hours
Seminar on Conducting a Successful Job Campaign

Training on Issues Associated With Relocation
Career Consultants of America offers a one-day training program to individuals who specialize in employee relocation. This program, entitled *The Psychological Aspects of Relocations: Improving Services and Cost Effectiveness,* enables managers to better attend to the psychological and support needs of individuals undergoing a relocation.

See reverse side for program outline.

100

The Psychological Aspects of Relocations: Improving Services and Cost Effectiveness

Program Outline

I. Introduction
   A. Relocation and the Family System: An Overview
   B. Statistics about Relocation
   C. Course Overview

II. Understanding the Psychological Aspects of Relocation
   A. Areas Affected
      1. Personal/Psychological Factors
      2. Career Issues
      3. Family Issues
         a. Dynamics among Spouses
         b. Children
         c. Community Attachments
      4. Logistical Factors
   B. Psychological/Behavioral Manifestations

III. Transferees and Their Needs
   A. The Dual Career Couple
   B. Relocations Involving Children
   C. Dealing with Angry Transferees
   D. Relocations with Complications

IV. Facilitating the Relocation
   A. Counseling Techniques
      1. Listening Skills
      2. Empathy
      3. Diagnosing Needs and Making Referrals
   B. Using Resources
      1. Community Resources
      2. Resources within the Organization
      3. Working with Relocation Professionals
   C. Facilitation Strategies
      1. Phase I: Before the Relocation
      2. Phase II: During the Relocation
      3. Phase III: After the Relocation and Beyond
   D. Developing and Implementing a Relocation Plan
   E. Exercise: Case Studies

- CCA's resources include; a) excellent network of local business leaders, including hundreds of local CCA alumni, b) library of resumes, directories, and other career resources, c) computer-based directory of Tampa Bay organizations from which individual searches are conducted, d) clerical sevices, e) video tape equipment for mock interviews, f) office space, g) referrals to a national network of certified career counselors, and h) computer-based guidance services.
- CCA has a very reputable corporate client list — both locally and nationally.
- A promotional piece sent to organizations interested in CCA's career guidance services for relocated spouses is shown in Figure 6-8.

Presented below is a telephone script CCA used to explore prospective clients' interest in outplacement services.

Sample Script Used to Gather Market Research Information On the Demand for Outplacement Services

Good morning/afternoon — my name is Sue Doe. I'm with Career Consultants of America and I'm conducting an industry study of over 200 Tampa-based organizations. I'd like to take about one minute of your time to ask you four brief questions about your organization's personnel policies. Are you the right person to be addressing my questions to? Good. Your responses will help local labor market professionals adopt strategies in line with industry trends.

First, has (Name of Organization) gone through a reorganization in the past six months?

Do you expect a reorganization in the next 6 months?

How many employees has (Name of Organization) redeployed — either through reorganization, changes in operations, or downsizings — since the beginning of the year?

How many employees do you plan to redeploy during the next six months?

Finally, does your organization offer employees outplacement services as part of their severance terms? If yes — How does your firm provide these services?; If no — Do you expect that your firm will be expanding its services in this area?

Thank you once again for your cooperation. Would you like a copy of the results of this study? (If yes, get name and address). Who else in your organization might be interested in a copy?

Organizational Career Development — CCA also offers organizations services in the areas of succession planning and employee development. Figure 6-9 displays an advertising piece which is sent to potential client organizations to solicit this type of business.

Figure 6-9 Organizational Career Development

Organizational Career Development

Reorganizations, acquisitions, mergers, and downsizings are contributing to an unprecedented number of personnel changes throughout American corporations. Talent that can both lead your organization through these transitions and, at the same time, keep it ahead of its competition is more in demand than ever.

Career Consultants of America can help your organization be sure it has the right people in the right places through succession planning and special career development programs.

Succession Planning

Strategic plans are the tools successful organizations use to plan and to communicate their visions . . . and employees bring these plans to life. Simply put, your organization's future is dependent upon your employees. It is the organization's task to identify, develop, and retain the talent it will need to realize its goals.

Organizational Career Development

Career Consultants of America assists organizations in drafting comprehensive succession plans. These plans are designed in synch with the organization's strategic plan, and incorporates needs assessments, career pathing, training and development plans, and comprehensive career development programming.

Experienced in succession planning with senior executives, mid-managers, fast trackers, minorities and special groups, Career Consultants of America can help your organization identify and plan to develop the talent it will need to master the challenges ahead.

Evaluation of Marketing Plan

It is vital to constantly analyze the effectiveness of the marketing plan to determine the pay-off of advertising expenditures and other resources devoted to the sales effort. It is recommended that at a minimum you track client inquiries and number of inquiries converted to clients by referral source for the various services offered by your practice.

In the case of services CCA offers to the community, the most inquiries were generated from television appearances and newspaper advertising. However, both of these sources had relatively low conversion to client ratios (both approximately 17%). The best conversion ratios were from referrals by former clients (77.3%), allied professionals (66.3%) and the local university (38.6%). Yellow pages advertising had a disappointing 9.5% conversion ratio. See Figure 6-10 for client sources for CCA during a recent year.

The analysis indicates that various types of referrals attract the majority of CCA career counseling clients. In order to make this type of analysis, good records must be kept, but it is well worth the effort so as to optimize your marketing plan.

Conclusion

A solid marketing plan can pay many long term dividends to the private practice career counselor. It is, in fact, critical to establishing your practice and to your practice's long term development. Being able to professionally package and market services of value to prospective clients, finding effective vehicles for gaining visibility and recognition as an expert practitioner, and continually monitoring and refining your marketing plan to capitalize on the most effective methods — these are the activities vital to growing your private practice. Above all, however, it is essential that the ethics associated with the counselor's marketing efforts are above reproach. This means that at times the counselor's responsibility is to *only* recommend services that are in the best interest of the prospective client. In addition, of course, this means that the counselor will also observe the ethical guidelines as outlined in Chapter 1.

My hope is that the sharing of the CCA marketing plan will help generate ideas for your practice.

Additional Thoughts on
"Professional Private Practice Marketing Considerations"

Shahnasarian — When clients come to me for career guidance I tell them that they will get in addition to the career counseling — access to a career library, receive a career newsletter, access to a computer-

Figure 6-10

Client Source for CCA

Referral Source	Percent of Clients
Spouse Relocation	16.1%
Client Referrals	15.2%
Local College Referrals	15.2%
T.V. Program Appearances	11.8%
Yellow Pages	5.9%
American Society for Training & Development Contacts	4.2%
Service Club Contacts	2.6%
NBCC Referrals	1.7%
Newspaper Ads	1.7%
All Other (Companies, magazines, etc.)	25.6%

assisted career guidance system, assessment instruments, etc. We maintain a file on employers in the area listing number of employees and names and telephone numbers of key personnel (network). Those that call our office asking for information about our services are encouraged to come in for an information session and 99% do this. We do not mail individual (retail) persons material as it discourages them from coming in for the information session. We have found very little interest in youth purchasing our career planning services. We have not found that traditional advertising has been very productive. Appearing on TV talk shows and discussing topics like career change and the work force 2000 has been worthwhile. Writing articles for local business publications has also paid off. My fee is $85/hour. There is no sliding scale. If the client cannot pay I have some free workshops. I will also make a referral to an appropriate agency. I do have a client follow-up after termination through several sources, my newsletter, work shops and group counseling.

Shepard — The office secretary handles calls relative to individual service and receives a 10% commission for every person she converts to a client. I handle the business and industry inquiries. The prospect

must pay for the initial discussion at the regular rate of $70/hour. This initial fee goes towards the subsequent package if this person becomes a client. The secretary calls business and industry firms and talks to the person in charge of training and personnel and sends them brochures. One week after sending the brochure the secretary calls back with the objective of setting up an appointment for me to go in and talk with them. The secretary obtains information relative to the firm on this call and I then write up a proposal for my services. I also run off a computer sheet to go with the proposal. In order to get referrals you must be very active in the community. People must have heard of you more than once. I offer a package of assessment instruments plus interpretation for $210. I never turn down a client, but my consulting work supports any free clients. Fee is never collected up front. My secretary works out a payment schedule with the client. If the client does not show up for an appointment there is no charge the first time. Thereafter, the client must pay for missed appointments. I offer a three month free follow up.

Musgrove — I do no consulting work nor run workshops. I do no advertising in the yellow pages, never write a proposal, and have no contracts. Career counseling clients come to me from the following sources:

Former client referrals	44%
Therapist referrals	20
Speeches I give to local organizations	9
Community sources	8
Former colleagues	7
Newspapers, radio, TV	4
Employment agencies and outplacement	2
Friends	2
Known client before	2
Yellow page listing	2

The career counselor must be absolutely committed to the client and have a passion for career counseling. Therapists are my second largest referral source. I invite them to lunch and talk about my career counseling work. My fee is $65/hour and there is no sliding scale. If the client cannot pay now they can come and pay later. After termination the secretary calls the client and asks the client for an evaluation of the service. The client is told there will be a free three month folow-up.

Hafer — I have done very little advertising. My charges are as follows; individual retail clients $50/session, company consulting $65/hour, and company outplacement $75/session/individual. Sessions frequently last more than one hour with the outplacement sessions being the longest. I have no sliding scale but have given some free career counseling to people who were out of work and referred by a church. It should be noted that an organization in Greenville named United Ministries (supported by churches and the United Way) does provide free job counseling to persons out of work. Referrals can be made to them in appropriate cases. Six months after the last counseling session a free follow-up session is offered.

I have found the most effective way to convert an inquirer into a client is to give a free information session to determine client needs and discuss services I would recommend to meet these needs. Past responses to telephone inquiries, plus mailing out information, has not been nearly as effective. Those who only call may be shopping for price and many of my competitors offer lower prices. There are five career counseling firms listed under "Career and Vocational Counseling" in the yellow pages in Greenville, plus one therapist also lists career counseling service. City population is 60,000 with another 60,000 in the immediate suburbs. It should be noted that the local community college has a Career Advancement Center with five full time career counselors devoted exclusively to non-students. Services and charges for this Career Advancement Center are extensively advertised throughout the area via mailings and newspaper ads. Services offered by this community college and charges include:

— Resume Preparation and Evaluation
  —Limited verbal critique of current resume — $10
  —Comprehensive resume including 20 copies, a sample cover letter and a thank-you letter with follow-up support and counseling — $65
— Videotape Inteviewing Services — $65
— Job Search Strategies — Class. Interviewing skills, networking techniques, resume preparation and researching employers — $65
— Career Testing, Interpretation and Consultation (interest inventory, personality indicator and values exercise) — $100
— Career and College Choices for High School Students (testing, interpretation and consultation) — $100

I have not done any newspaper or direct mail advertising. In a recent year the source of my career counseling clients has been as follows:

Source	*Percent of Clients*
Employment Agency Referrals	23%
Mental Health Counselor Referrals	18
Previous Client Referrals	18
Yellow Pages (listing - no ad)	13
Business Referrals	5
Other Referrals (Friends, Churches, Clubs, etc.)	23

Chapter Seven — How to Start a Private Practice

Frank Karpati
Career Directions
Hackensack, NJ

Introduction

Establishing a career counseling private practice is a major task combining extensive planning with substantial personal and financial commitment.

Although, as counselors we are dedicated to helping people make better educated career choices, we should not lose sight of the fact that in private practice we are in a business. In the United States 96% of all new businesses fail. Most new businesses fail because of poor management and lack of sufficient financing. Therefore, establishing a private practice is not for everyone. As a matter of fact it is not for most. Also, since most career counselors are working in nonprofit settings, crossing the bridge into the business world will likely require adjustment in one's value system and additional training in management, finance and marketing.

An examination of the literature on marketing of professional services reveals that it focuses on the management of an existing practice. Therefore, in this section, we would like to review some of the steps necessary to conceptually and operationally develop a successful new private practice.

Market Potential

Before making any type of financial commitment to a private practice, examine the market potential, existing private practices and other competition, and projected economics and population growth.

Focus of Practice

Upon evaluating demographic factors and determining a void in the market, meticulous attention should be given to sculpturing a specialty to properly address the needs of the community, while optimizing the correlation between your expertise and market needs.

Financial Investment and Operating Expenses

Since most career counselors are not financially independent, sensible financial and budgetary planning is essential so as not to underestimate capital expenditures and operating costs. Cash flow is one of the greatest pitfalls of a private practice. In this section, we will assess the financial feasibility of establishing the practice and provide you with some administrative tools that proved to be beneficial in managing successful practices. After carefully assessing and evaluating your costs, fill in Figure 7-1, Annual Budget Planning Expenses. Under

ADVERTISING category, determine in which near-by cities you may list your office phone and the type of yellow page ads you plan to purchase. Figure 7-2, Yellow Pages Planning Sheet may help in this connection. Figure 7-2 targets a number of near-by cities with the office phone listed under three major headings, i.e., ''Educational Consulting'' (Ed.Cons.), ''Resume'' and ''Career Counseling.'' Call your Yellow Pages representative several weeks before the books close and request pricing information for the telephone books you would like to appear in. Evaluate your budget, competitive activities and determine the size of the ads. After you have filled out a table similar to Figure 7-2, transcribe the costs onto Figure 7-1. Call your local telephone company to obtain costs for the different telephone services you are considering, in addition to the ads. Some telephone services you may want to consider include call forwarding and call interrupt. Business telephone costs can be substantial and your estimate should include installation charges, monthly fees, and long distance charges. These costs should be filled in under ''TELEPHONE'' on Figure 7-1. Do not sign a contract for your telephone advertising and services until you are satisfied that the estimated total expenses can be supported by the estimated business income.

Based upon the focus of your practice, competitor activities, and available resources, set up a planned mailing schedule for potential referral organizations and print media to optimize your market penetration. Enter these costs on Figure 7-1 under ADVERTISING, ''Other Printed Material'' and ''Mailing/Postage.''

Estimated attorney and accountant costs can be included under ''Outside Contractors'' on Figure 7-1. If you are going to incorporate your business you will probably need help from an attorney. You may decide initially to not incorporate even though personal financial liability may be greater. Also be sure you understand tax (federal and state) and FICA implications of being incorporated and not being incorporated. An accountant can provide this information.

Figure 7-1   Annual Budget Planning Expenses

ANNUAL BUDGET PLANNING EXPENSES
PROFESSIONAL/BUSINESS EXPENSES

ADVERTISING
Yellow Pages _____
Other Printed Material _____
Mailing/Postage _____
Total $ _____

AUTOMOBILE
Purchase _____
Depreciation _____
Insurance/Registration _____
Repairs/Maintenance _____
Fuel _____
Total $ _____

PROFESSIONAL
MEMBERSHIPS AND DUES
Total $ _____

PUBLICATIONS
Library _____
Depreciation _____
Total $ _____

INSURANCES
Professional Liability _____
Health Insurance _____
Disability Insurance _____
Total $ _____

BUSINESS TRAVEL
Air Transportation _____
Ground Transportation _____
Lodging _____
Meals _____
Miscellaneous _____
Total $ _____

RENT
Total _____

UTILITIES
Gas & Electric _____
Water _____
Total $ _____

OUTSIDE CONTRACTORS
Administrative Services _____
Consultants & Training _____
Total $ _____

SUPPLIES
Software _____
Supplies _____
Printing _____
Total $ _____

OFFICE EQUIPMENT
Service Contracts _____
Computer _____
Depreciation _____
Fax Machine _____
Depreciation _____
Laser Printer _____
Depreciation _____
Copiers _____
Depreciation _____
Total $ _____

OFFICE FURNITURE
Desks _____
Depreciation _____
Chairs _____
Depreciation _____
Filing Cabinet _____
Depreciation _____
Other _____
Total $ _____

TELEPHONE
Office _____
Home _____
Total $ _____

PUBLIC RELATIONS/
ENTERTAINMENT
Total $ _____

Figure 7-2   Yellow Pages Planning Sheet

YELLOW PAGES PLANNING SHEET

YEAR _____

LIST OF YELLOW PAGES

PLACED
- ED. CONSULTANT
- RESUME SERVICES
- CAREER COUNSELING
- BOLD LINE
- ADDITIONAL LINE
- 1/2" AD
- 1" AD
- 1 1/2" RED AD

PRICING
- 1/16" PAGE — B&W / RED / COLOR
- 1/8" PAGE — B&W / RED / COLOR

Office rent, Figure 7-1, can be a major expense. Normally a one year's lease is required. A longer lease may result in a lower monthly rental, but is not recommended until your business is well established. Keep in mind that a lease is a financial obligation that must be paid whether you are making money or not, or even still using the space.

Initial office equipment (see Figure 7-1, OFFICE EQUIPMENT) can be a sizeable investment. Whether you will want to immediately procure a computer and copier is a major decision. You may elect to farm out this work initially. In the long run an IBM compatible microcomputer with good software packages for at least word processing, data management and accounting should permit the business to function efficiently. Addition later of a desk top publisher can facilitate a newsletter for potential customers and referral sources.

Although not shown on Figure 7-1, you will need to decide if you are going to pay yourself a salary and allow for income taxes, state workers's compensation and IRS FICA. Do you plan to hire a secretary/receptionist in the first year or will you subcontract these services? If you plan to subcontract these services then add these expenses under OUTSIDE CONTRACTORS "Administrative Services" in Figure 7-1.

In order to satisfy the IRS, you also need to keep good business expense records. Suggested forms are shown in Figure 7-3. Monitoring and recording of daily expenses ("Entertainment," "Local," "Mileage," and "Out of Town" travel) is an important function that is overlooked by most new businesses. Make sure you complete these forms daily so that you can claim all appropriate expenses. Transcribe these expenses weekly or monthly into the proper categories contained in Figure 7-1 so that you can compare actual expenses to your budget on a monthly basis.

Client Records

Update the Monthly Bookkeeping client records form, Figure 7-4, after each client session. This will provide current client records and permit a monthly analysis of referral agencies. Based upon this analysis you can then upgrade your marketing program, e.g., if no clients are resulting from a particular advertising or yellow pages program, then drop these ineffective sources.

You may also want to utilize a formal counseling agreement with your clients relative to the scope of your services, charges and the client's obligations. Figure 7-5 and Figure 7-6 show typical examples of the counselor/client agreement. This agreement should indicate the services provided, charge for each session, what the session and services entail, and the client's responsibility. Your particular agreement should be approved by attorney to ensure that it is compatible with state laws and will be enforceable on your part if this becomes necessary.

Figure 7-3 Log of Expenses

LOG OF EXPENSES

BUSINESS EXPENSES

ENTERTAINMENT		AMOUNT	
WHO:	LUNCH		
BUSINESS PURPOSE:	DINNER		
WHERE:			
	OTHER		
	TOTAL		

LOCAL		
PARKING/TOLLS		
TOTAL		

MILEAGE LOG		
TOTAL MILES		
PERSONAL MILES		
BUSINESS MILES		

ENTERTAINMENT		AMOUNT	
WHO:	LUNCH		
BUSINESS PURPOSE:	DINNER		
WHERE:	HOME		
	OTHER		
	TOTAL		

LOCAL		
PARKING/TOLLS		
TOTAL		

MILEAGE LOG		
TOTAL MILES		
PERSONAL MILES		
BUSINESS MILES		

ENTERTAINMENT		AMOUNT	
WHO:	LUNCH		
BUSINESS PURPOSE:	DINNER		
WHERE:	HOME		
	OTHER		
	TOTAL		

LOCAL		
PARKING/TOLLS		
TOTAL		

MILEAGE LOG		
TOTAL MILES		
PERSONAL MILES		
BUSINESS MILES		

ENTERTAINMENT		AMOUNT	
WHO:	LUNCH		
BUSINESS PURPOSE:	DINNER		
WHERE:	HOME		
	OTHER		
	TOTAL		

LOCAL		
PARKING/TOLLS		
TOTAL		

MILEAGE LOG		
TOTAL MILES		
PERSONAL MILES		
BUSINESS MILES		

114

TRAVEL EXPENSES

OUT-OF-TOWN		
WHERE:	BREAKFAST	
	LUNCH	
	DINNER	
	HOTEL	
BUSINESS PURPOSE:	TRAVEL	
	AUTO LEASE	
	PARKING/TOLLS	
	TOTAL	

OUT-OF-TOWN		
WHERE:	BREAKFAST	
	LUNCH	
	DINNER	
	HOTEL	
BUSINESS PURPOSE:	TRAVEL	
	AUTO LEASE	
	PARKING/TOLLS	
	TOTAL	

OUT-OF-TOWN		
WHERE:	BREAKFAST	
	LUNCH	
	DINNER	
	HOTEL	
BUSINESS PURPOSE:	TRAVEL	
	AUTO LEASE	
	PARKING/TOLLS	
	TOTAL	

OUT-OF-TOWN		
WHERE:	BREAKFAST	
	LUNCH	
	DINNER	
	HOTEL	
BUSINESS PURPOSE:	TRAVEL	
	AUTO LEASE	
	PARKING/TOLLS	
	TOTAL	

115

Figure 7-4   Monthly Bookkeeping

MONTHLY BOOKKEEPING

DATE	CLIENT	REFERRED		PAYMENT	TO DATE	SERVICES	

02 06 1 9 004 (8 10)

116

Figure 7-5 Client/Counselor Agreement Form

Frank S. Karpati, M.A., N.C.C., R.P.C., N.C.C.C., ABVE-Diplomate
Executive Director

Nationally Certified Counselor
Registered Professional Counselor
Nationally Certified Career Counselor
Certified Academic Counselor
American Board of Vocational Experts-Diplomate

AGREEMENT

I, _____ , agree to utilize the counseling and/or consulting
services with the full understanding that the firm will act in an advisory capacity and will in no
way be liable for my career and/or academic direction or success. The Career Counseling process is
outlined on the flow chart below.

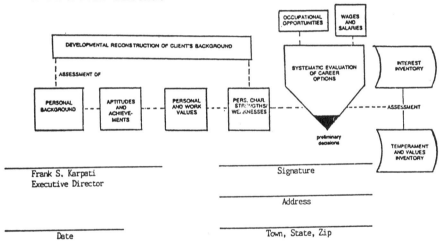

Frank S. Karpati
Executive Director

_____
Signature

_____
Address

_____
Date

_____
Town, State, Zip

FEE SCHEDULE

The fee for a 70-120 minute consultation is $ 165.00 payable at the time of the conference. This
fee also includes counselor research, preparation and testing services. Therefore, for the fee the
client should expect to receive 2-1/2 to 3 hours of professional services. Although the exact
number of sessions cannot be initially determined, counseling is usually completed within three to
five sessions.

In order for the counseling service to maintain its ability to function and provide the servies you
need, it is necessary to require of all clients that they be responsible for the time set aside for
their consultation. This is particularly essential since a counselor's time is allotted to you
alone for the duration of your session, and cannot be used in any other way. In the event that
illness or emergency prevents your coming for counseling, you must notify the agency at least 24
hours in advance. The counselor will be happy to discuss this matter with you at length if you
deem it appropriate.

rev. 1989

28 Summit Avenue   Hackensack, New Jersey 07601-1263   (201) 487-0808
Services are conducted in accordance with APA and AACD Ethical Standards

Figure 7-6   Client/Counselor Resume Agreement Form

Frank S. Karpatl, M.A., N.C.C., N.J.C.C., N.C.C.C., ABVE-Diplomate
Executive Director   National Certified Counselor
New Jersey Certified Counselor
National Certified Career Counselor
Certified Academic Counselor
American Board of Vocational Experts-Diplomate

AGREEMENT

I, _____, agree to utilize the resume
developing services of Career Directions with the full understanding
that the firm will develop the resume with the editorial assistance
of the client and will _not_ assist with either job placement or career
decision-making.

PROCESS

Client receives a quote, without obligation, for the resume services.
If the quote is acceptable, the purpose of the _first session_ is to
gather all appropriate career and personal information. The
approximate time to gather this information is 45 minutes to one (1)
hours. In preparation for the _second session_, the counselor will
draft a copy of the resume. The resume draft will then be presented
in a typed format to allow the client to more effectively assess, not
only content, but the final visual layout. During the second
session, the client, with the assistance of the counselor, will edit
the resume, and at the culmination of the session, when the client
feels comfortable with the contents of the resume, will approve the
resume for printing.

PICK-UP POLICY

Resumes will be picked up during regular working hours. We assume _no_
responsibility for resumes or any other printed matter not picked-up
within _thirty_ days of date below.

FEES

A half deposit is required at the end of the _first_ session, with
balance due at the end of the second session. Final payment _must_ be
certified check or cash. Receipts will be provided upon request.

Objective
of Resume _____

Approved _____ copies on _____ stock. Price: $_____

_____   _____   _____
Client's Signature   Date   Frank S. Karpati
                                                     Executive Director

118

Client Material

If you are a National Certified Career Counselor you will want to give your clients a copy of the *Consumer Guidelines for Selecting a Career Counselor,* Figure 7-7. You can also give your clients a copy of the NBCC *Counseling Services: Consumer Rights and Responsibilities* shown in Figure 7-8. Bulk quantities of this sheet may be ordered from the National Board for Certified Counselors.

Career counselors are approached by perspective clients for a multitude of reasons. If career counseling is inappropriate for any number of reasons, the counselor should make a referral, unless competent in the appropriate area. Reasons for this referral should be discussed with the client. A written release should be obtained from the client prior to providing information, assessment instruments, etc., to the referred source. If the career counselor needs information from the client's previous mental or physical health specialist, the release form shown in Figure 7-9 should be signed by the client and forwarded to the appropriate individual.

Resource Document

Career counselors contemplating establishing a private practice should secure and read carefully the NCDA publication, *The Professional Practice of Career Counseling and Consultation: A Resource Document* (1988), Figure 7-10. This document can be very helpful in assisting the counselor in defining his/her role functions and determining the focus of the practice.

Counseling Resources

If you are presently working in a public career counseling setting, the likelihood that you will have to modify your present counseling practices is almost certain. When clients are paying for professional services, they usually have different expectations. Anyone planning to go into private practice should conduct a comprehensive literature survey of state-of-the-art practices, assessment instruments and counseling resources. Based on your theoretical orientation and the focus of your practice, design services to properly address the needs of your clients.

Office

Initial impressions are important. Selection of site and decoration of your office should be given careful consideration. Office should be centrally located and easily accessible by public transportation.

Figure 7-7 Consumer Guidelines for Selecting a Career Counselor

National Career Development Association

Founded in 1913 as the National Vocational Guidance Association

A Division of the AMERICAN ASSOCIATION FOR COUNSELING AND DEVELOPMENT

5999 Stevenson Avenue / Alexandria, VA 22304 / AC 703 823-9800

Consumer Guidelines for Selecting A Career Counselor

Sometimes it seems that virtually everyone is a vocational coach, ready and anxious to give advice, suggestions, and directions. Unfortunately, all are not equally able to provide the kind of help persons need in making decisions about what to do with their lives. Promises and luxurious trappings are poor substitutes for competency. Thus, the selection of a professional career counselor is a very important task. The following guidelines are offered to assist you in making this selection.

Credentials of the Professional Career Counselor

A Nationally Certified Career Counselor (NCCC) signifies that the career counselor has achieved the highest certification in the profession. Further, it means that the career counselor has:

- earned a graduate degree in counseling or in a related professional field from a regionally accredited higher education institution
- completed supervised counseling experience which included career counseling
- acquired a minimum of three years of full-time career development work experience
- obtained written endorsements of competence in career counseling from a work supervisor and a professional colleague
- successfully completed a knowledge-based certification examination
- other professional counselors may be trained in one or two year counselor preparation programs with specialities in career counseling and may be licensed or certified by national or state professional associations

What Do Career Counselors Do?

The services of career counselors differ, depending on competence. A professional or Nationally Certified Career Counselor helps people make decisions and plans related to life/career directions. The strategies and techniques are tailored to the specific needs of the person seeking help. It is likely that the career counselor will do one or more of the following:

- conduct individual and group personal counseling sessions to help clarify life/career goals
- administer and interpret tests and inventories to assess abilities, interests, etc. and to identify career options
- encourage exploratory activities through assignments and planning experiences

- utilize planning systems and occupational information systems to help individuals better understand the world of work
- provide opportunities for improving decision-making skills
- assist in developing individualized career plans
- teach job hunting strategies and skills and assist in the development of resumes
- help resolve potential personal conflicts on the job through practice in human relations skills
- assist in understanding the integration of work and other life roles
- provide support for persons experiencing job stress, job loss, career transition

Ask for a detailed explanation of services (career counseling, testing, employment search strategy planning and resume writing). Make sure you understand the service, your degree of involvement and financial commitment.

Fees

Select a counselor who is professionally trained and will let you choose the services you desire. Make certain you can terminate the services at any time, paying only for services rendered.

Promises

Be skeptical of services that make promises of more money, better jobs, resumes that get speedy results or an immediate solution to career problems.

Ethical Practices

A Professional or Nationally Certified Career Counselor is expected to follow ethical guidelines of such organizations as The National Career Development Association, The American Association for Counseling and Development, and The American Psychological Association. Professional codes of ethics advise against grandiose guarantees and promises, exorbitant fees, and breaches of confidentiality, among other things. You may wish to ask for a detailed explanation of services offered, your financial and time commitments, and a copy of the ethical guidelines used by the career counselor you are considering.

These guidelines were adopted by the NCCC Committee and approved by the Board of Directors of the National Career Development Association.

Compliments of

**Figure 7-8   Counseling Services: Consumer Rights
and Responsibilities**

Counseling Services:
Consumer Rights and Responsibilities

Consumer Rights

- Be informed of the qualifications of your counselor: education, experience, and professional counseling certification(s) and state license(s).
- Receive an explanation of services offered, your time commitments, and fee scales and billing policies prior to receipt of services.
- Be informed of limitations of the counselor's practice to special areas of expertise (e.g., career development, ethnic groups, etc.) or age group (e.g., adolescents, older adults, etc.).
- Have all that you say treated confidentially and be informed of any state laws placing limitations on confidentiality in the counseling relationship.
- Ask questions about the counseling techniques and strategies and be informed of your progress.
- Participate in setting goals and evaluating progress toward meeting them.
- Be informed of how to contact the counselor in an emergency situation.
- Request referral for a second opinion at any time.
- Request copies of records and reports to be used by other counseling professionals.
- Receive a copy of the code of ethics to which your counselor adheres.
- Contact the appropriate professional organization if you have doubts or complaints relative to the counselor's conduct.
- Terminate the counseling relationship at any time.

Consumer Responsibilities

- Set and keep appointments with your counselor. Let him/her know as soon as possible if you cannot keep an appointment.
- Pay your fees in accordance with the schedule you preestablished with the counselor.
- Help plan your goals.
- Follow through with agreed -pon goals.
- Keep your counselor informed of your progress toward meeting your goals.
- Terminate your counseling relationship before entering into arrangements with another counselor.

This statement was prepared jointly by the National Board for Certified Counselors and Chi Sigma Iota to help you understand and exercise your rights as a consumer of counseling services. NBCC and CSI believe that clients who are informed consumers are able to best use counseling services to meet their individual needs.

Compliments of

Figure 7-9   Release Form

CAREER DIRECTIONS

Frank S. Karpati, M.A., N.C.C., R.P.C., N.C.C.C., ABVE-Diplomate
Executive Director

Nationally Certified Counselor
Registered Professional Counselor
Nationally Certified Career Counselor
Certified Academic Counselor
American Board of Vocational Experts-Diplomate

RELEASE FORM

I, _____ grant

permission to _____

to discuss with Frank S. Karpati my personal background

and information gathered during the professional consultation

and/or therapy session(s) in order to allow Frank S. Karpati

to more effectively assist me with my career counseling and

planning.

Frank S. Karpati	Client's Signature
	Street
	Town/City State Zip

_____
Date

28 Summit Avenue   Hackensack, New Jersey 07601-1263   (201) 487-0808
Services are conducted in accordance with APA and AACD Ethical Standards

THE PROFESSIONAL PRACTICE OF CAREER

COUNSELING AND CONSULTATION:

A RESOURCE DOCUMENT

published by

The National Career Development Association

(Founded in 1913 as the National Vocational Guidance Association)

January, 1988

A Division of the American Association for Counseling and Development

5999 Stevenson Avenue/Alexandria, VA 22304/AC 703 823-9800

Marketing

Marketing is a complex task requiring continuous attention assessing market trends, competitor activities and monitoring the effectiveness of individual advertising programs. If a program does not produce the desired results, it should be eliminated.

Reaching Your Potential Clients

Patience is a virtue. If you sign a contract with Yellow Pages today, it could take several months to over a year before the public sees your ad. The annual cut-off date for the Yellow Pages varies from region to region. Therefore you should contact your Yellow Pages Representative for this information. If you send a mailing to potential referral services (e.g., psychologists, attorneys, physical therapists, employment agencies) the likelihood that you will receive referrals right away is minimal. Introducing yourself over the phone and sending a personal note usually is more effective. In the long run,

the best referral source is former clients. Therefore, staying in touch with former clients is not only a courtesy, but also good business.

If you are interested in developing a corporate career development practice, in all likelihood, it will take an even longer period of time. Many corporations do not provide career development assistance. Even those that do, like most large organizations, tend to be bureaucratic and plan and execute slowly. Therefore, establish realistic time lines to project cash flow reliably.

Legal Contracts, Insurance and Accounting

Selecting the right professionals can aid you immeasurably in coping with the turbulence of establishing a private practice. Developing agreements with clients and reviewing contracts should be done by an attorney who has extensive expertise in this area.

Although the cost of professional and personal liability insurance at first glance appears to be high, and most of us are tempted to save money, this is not the place to cut costs. Keep in mind that AACD offers members liability insurance. Upon completing the annual budget summary form, and overcoming the shock from the bottom line, the realization of need for financial planning and development of an efficient accounting system becomes apparent. After developing your business plans, select an accountant who specializes in providing services to private professional service organizations.

Partnership

The beginning of any private practice is a learning experience which has its ups and downs. Since most small businesses fail, and you are repeatedly faced with unknowns, selecting a partner, unless you have a long working relationship with the colleague, is not advisable. If a partnership is unavoidable, minimize misunderstandings by carefully documenting obligations and responsibilities of each partner. This should take the form of a legal document reviewed by an attorney and signed by each partner. Building up a private practice takes time and negative cash flow can strain the professional relationship.

Burnout

As stated repeatedly, the development of a successful practice takes an enormous amount of effort, cost and personal sacrifice. We have known for some time that human services professionals are in considerable danger of experiencing stress and burnout. So, a word of caution: maintain a healthy balance between personal and professional life.

Additional Thoughts on "How to Start a Private Practice"

Hafer — In most cases it is best to "ease into" a career counseling private practice unless, for example, your previous contacts have resulted in commitments from several companies to use your services in consulting, outplacement, or spousal relocation. The safest way to start is to retain your current employment and start a part-time practice with evening and weekend hours. Do not over commit relative to expenses. Things to consider include:

1. Office space — you can get along with about 150 square feet if you will initially have no help. Do not sign a lease for longer than one year.

2. Telephone — minimum business service with call forwarding will be about $60/month. This will give you one listing in the yellow pages under "Career and Vocational Counseling" and one line in the business section. A telephone answering machine is a practical way of maintaining communications with the outside world during counseling sessions and when you are not in the office.

3. Office career resource library — determine what college catalogues, Department of Labor publications, and other counseling material you will need initially. See the Appendix for more on this subject.

4. Assessment instruments — decide which assessment instruments, if any, you will use. See Chapter Five for more on this subject.

5. Office furniture — What are your requirements? What will it cost?

6. Certifications — You will have more credibility if you become an NCCC. If your state has licensure or registration obtain these credentials also.

7. Office services — Determine how you will handle typing and reproduction. If you plan to offer resume service, where will you get the professional appearing printing done? A laser printer is recommended.

8. Counseling Charges — What will you charge for various types of service? See Chapter Six for more on this topic. Research your potential competition including types of service and charges.

9. Brochures and busines cards — Decide what you will initially need and get printed.

10. Advertising — What advertising will you initially use and what will the costs be?

I know one case where a counselor quit her job, took a three year lease on a three room office suite, bought a microcomputer, took out ads in both the yellow pages and the consolidated phone book but lasted only nine months before folding the business.It is prudent to have enough financial resources to last two years with minimal personal salary and business income as you establish your counseling business.

Appendix — The Private Practice
Career Resource Library

Al A. Hafer

This annotated bibliography is added to assist career counselors in private practice in finding additional resource material. This appendix is aimed at accomplishing this objective and to also indicate the type of material that is included in a private practice career library. A brief description of the contents of items in my career resource library is included in brackets after the item. Those items marked with an "*" after the first word are the minimal resource list that should be available at the start of a private practice.

Career Counseling Library Material

A counselor's guide to education and training opportunities in the Air Force. (1985). Washington DC: United States Government Printing Office. [Information about the Air Force including education programs, commissioning opportunities, scholarships and technical training.]

Academic preparation for the world of work. (1984). New York: College Board Publications. [Basic academic competencies, computer competency, on-the-job behavior and attitudes, and studying.]

Allen, J.G. (1985). *How to turn an interview into a job.* Des Moines, IA: Simon & Schuster Audio. [This is a 52 minute audio tape which discusses writing a resume, a cover letter, preparing for an interview and job search suggestions.]

Allied health education directory. (1989). Chicago: American Medical Association. [Listing of post secondary institutions that offer technician, technology and therapist training in the health field. Describes job content and accreditation.]

Anastasi, A. (1976). *Psychological testing.* NY: MacMillan Publishing Co. [One of the most widely used counselor graduate level text books. All career counselors should have this as a reference source.]

ASVAB: A brief guide for counselors and educators. (1986). Washington, DC: U.S. Government Printing Office. [Provides key information on The Armed Services Vocational Aptitude Battery, a multiple aptitude test offered free of charge to students in secondary and post-secondary schools.]

Azrin, N.H., & Besalel, V.A. (1980). *Job club counselor's manual: A behavioral approach to vocational counseling.* Baltimore: University Park Press. [How to organize, set up and start a job club. Establish the goal, develop procedures and activities, writing the cover letter, resume, interview, behavioral approach to job counseling, forms to use in club.]

Beatty, R. (1991). *Get the right job in 60 days or less.* NY: John Wiley & Sons. [Good basic job search book.]

Birsner, E.P. (1991). *The 40+ job hunting guide.* New York: Facts on File. [Job search tips for the older worker.]

Blake, R.R., & Mouton, J.S. (1964). *The managerial grid.* Houston: Gulf Publishing Co. [A comprehensive book relative to mobilizing human effort and for getting maximum performance results from industrial profcssional cmployees. Includes managerial theories and facades and deceptive strategies.]

Bloch, D.P. (1990). *How to make the right career moves.* Lincolnwood, IL: VGM Career Horizons. [Evaluating where you are, performance reviews, rating worksheets, evaluating current job satisfaction, moving ahead in your career where you are and moving out, finding the right job, resume and interviews.]

Bloch, D.P. (1988). *How to get and get ahead on your first job.* Lincolnwood, IL: VGM Career Horizons. [Information on finding and getting ahead on a person's first job. Covers job applications, resumes, cover letters, interviewing, job search and includes many work sheets.]

Bolles, R.N. (1979). *The quick job-hunting map: A fast way to help.* [A workbook for identifying your basic skills, where to use your skills, how to identify the kind of job you want, identify the kind of organizations which have that sort of job and how to get hired there. According to the workbook 86% of the people using it get the job and in shorter time.]

Bolles, R.N. (1991). *What Color is your parachute?: A practical manual for job-hunters & career changers.* Berkeley, CA: Ten Speed Press. [Comprehensive career and job hunting information including self assessment, impact of getting fired, resumes, interviewing, job search techniques, etc.]

Bradley, J. (1982). *Making smart career decisions.* Pomona, CA: Focus on the Family. [Audio tape CS 125 — discusses relationship of natural gifts and talents to career, as well as burnout.]

Bradley, L.J. (1990). *Counseling midlife career changers.* Garrett Park, MD: Garrett Park Pres. [Discusses approach and things to consider in counseling adults who are considering a career change. This is one of NCDA's "How to do it" books.]

Brown, S.T., & Brown, D. (1990). *Designing and implementing a career information center.* Garrett Park, MD: Garrett Park Press. [Contains detailed information on how to set up a career information center and resources to include. This is one of NCDA's "How to do it" books.]

Business Week's guide to careers: Job search workshop. New York: McGraw Hill. [Self-Evaluation exercises, resumes, interviews, a guidebook to a video vignette on job search.]

Campbell, D.P. (1974). *If you don't know where you're going, you'll probably end up somewhere else.* Allen, TX: Argus Communications. [A book for adolescents aimed at getting them to think realistically about their careers. It uses Holland's occupational/personality typologies.]

Career education wall charts. Garrett Park, MD: Garrett Park Press. [Set of 25 charts, 17 x 22'', which deal with job search methods, outlook in career fields, myths about employment, etc.]

Career opportunities news (periodical). Garrett Park, MD: Garrett Park Press. [Issued six times each year summarizes occupational trends, career items of interest to minorities and women, new career publications, and sources of free and inexpensive career materials].

Career World. Northbrook, IL: General Learning Corporation. [A career magazine, aimed at adolescents, which is published monthly from September through May. Features many different occupations.]

Carney, C.G., Wells, C.F., & Streufert, D. (1981). *Career planning: Skills to build your future.* Monterey, CA: Brooks/Cole Publishing CO. [A college text for use in a college career planning course. Includes removing attitudinal blocks to career decision making, reconstruction process, making career decisions, self assessment, adult life stages.]

Centi, P. (1981). *Up with the positive, out with the negative.* Englewood Cliffs, NJ: Prentice-Hall, Inc. [The author, a director of a college counseling center, discusses negative self-concepts and self-perceptions that do people harm by underestimating a person's real merit or worthiness.]

Changing images: Career models in the 80s. The Women's Development Center, Greenville Technical College. Greenville, SC: DOORWAY Publishers. [Book presents examples of persons who have successfully entered 50 different vocations traditionally reserved for members of the opposite sex. Occupations range from bus driver to executive vice president.]

College facts chart: For students, parents and guidance counselors. (1988-89). Spartanburg, SC: National Beta Club. [Information on 3488 post secondary educational institutions in the United States by state.]

College/University Catalogs — a selection from institutions in my state and nearby states.

 *Counselor's manual for the armed services vocational aptitude battery form 14.* (1989). Washington, DC: U.S. Government Printing Office. [Detailed instructions on how to administer and interpret the ASVAB. Includes information on norming sample, reliability and validity of the ASVAB.]

CPC annual: A directory of employment opportunities for college graduates in administration, business, and other nontechnical options. Volume 2. (annual). Bethlehem, PA: College Placement Council, Inc. [Employment opportunities for college graduates in administration, business and other nontechnical careers.]

CPC annual: A directory of employment opportunities for college graduates in engineering sciences, the computer field, and other technical options. Volume 3. (annual). Bethlehem, PA: College Placement Council, Inc. [Employment opportunities for college graduates with degrees in technical disciplines, e.g., engineering, science and computer science.]

CPC annual: A guide to career planning, the job search, graduate school, and work-related education. Volume 1. (annual). Bethlehem, PA: College Placement Council, Inc. [How to research companies, interviewing, job search, how to apply for government jobs.]

DeRosis, H.A., & Pellegrino, V.Y. (1977). *The book of hope: How women can overcome depression.* NY: Bantam Books. [The reviewer of this book suggests that it is a primer on depression for women and men, and for the layman and professional.]

Derr, C.B. (1988). *Managing the new careerists.* San Francisco: Jossey-Bass Publishers. [Describes the five distinct career orientations, the Career Success Map Questionnaire, identifies career transition points and suggests applications of this concept for career counselors.]

Derr, C.B. (1989). *Career success map: Recognizing and achieving your career aspirations.* San Francisco: Jossey-Bass Publishers. [Two audio tapes that discuss Dr. Derr's five career orientations, i.e., Getting Ahead, Getting Secure, Getting Free, Getting High and Getting Balanced. Useful in assisting clients to determine desired career orientation.]

Dictionary of occupational titles: Fourth edition supplement*. (1986). Washington, DC: U.S. Department of Labor, Employment and Training Administration. [Lists new occupations defined by the DOL since the 1977 edition including the DOT codes.]

Dictionary of occupational titles*. (1977). Washington, DC: United States Department of Labor, Employment, and Training Administration. [A concise definition of about 20,000 jobs, listing the DOT nine digit code.]

Doughty, H.R. (1990). *Guide to American graduate schools.* NY: Penguin Books. [Contains information on the accredited graduate schools in the U.S. including degrees, entrance requirements, courses of study, etc.]

Encyclopedia of careers and vocational guidance. (1990). Chicago: J. G. Ferguson Publishing Company. [Four volume set which summarizes work and outlook in a number of occupations. Fourth volume deals with technician careers.]

Eskelin, N. (1980). *Yes yes living in a no no world.* Plainfield, NJ: Logos International. [The author indicates that in every situation a person can respond with hope instead of fear, with encouragement instead of criticism, and with belief instead of despair.]

Exploring careers: The world of work and you. (1990-1991). Indianapolis, IN: JIST Works, Inc. [Written for junior high school age students. Includes a work values exercise. Lists 19 job characteristics and matches them to 300 occupations from the *Occupational Outlook Handbook.*]

Farr, J.M. (1988). *Getting the job you really want.* Indianapolis: JIST Works, Inc. [What employers look for, self evaluation exercises to set future goals, critical and transferable skills, power skills, evaluating skills, job matching chart, job hunting techniques, networking, employment applications, interview, resume, cover letter, instructor's guide also available for this book.]

Gelott, H.B. (1990). *Positive uncertainty: An empowering approach to career decision making.* Alexandria, VA: National Career Development Association. [This is an audio tape of a presentation made at the 1990 National Conference of the NCDA at Scottsdale, AZ.]

Getting the right job. (1987). New York: American Telephone and Telegraph. [A brief review for college students as to how to get a job. Includes targeting a career, resume, cover letter, job search, and interviewing.]

Gordon, V.N. (1984). *The undecided college student: An academic & career advising challenge.* Springfield, IL: Charles C. Thomas, Publisher. [Provides insight as to why some college students are educationally and vocationally undecided, and career development concepts for reducing career indecision.]

Gottfredson*, G.D., & Holland, J.L. (1989). *Dictionary of Holland occupational codes.* (2nd Edition). Odessa, FL: Psychological Assessment Resources, Inc. [Listing of 12,860 occupational titles along with the DOT codes and Holland Codes. If you plan to use the Holland typologies you should have this publication.]

Gysbers, N.C., & Associates (Ed.). (1986). *Designing careers: Counseling to enhance education, work, and leisure.* San Francisco: Jossey-Bass, Inc. [Book initially published by NCDA on the occasion of the 70th anniversary of NVGA. Examines major developments in theory and practice during preceding decade and points the direction for vocational guidance in 80s.]

Handbook of trade & technical careers & training. Washington, DC: National Association of Trade & Technical Schools. [Listing of accredited National Association of Trade and Technical Schools. 98 careers you can learn in two years or less and schools that provide the necessary training. Description of job and how to choose a trade school.]

Hansen*, J.C. (1989). *User's guide for the SVIB-SII: Strong interest inventory.* Palo Alto, CA: Consulting Psychologists Press. [Guidelines for counselors in understanding and interpreting the SII. Includes reliability and validity information. If you plan to use the SII you need this.]

Herr, E.L., & Cramer, S.H. (1988). *Career guidance and counseling through the life span: Systematic approaches.* Glenview, IL: Scott Foresman and Company. [A graduate level career counseling text book. Comprehensive coverage of career counseling theories, computer assisted career guidance systems, assessment instruments, etc.]

Holmes, A.F. (1984). *Ethics: Approaching moral decisions.* Downers Grove, IL: InterVarsity Press. [This book discusses Christian ethics applied to four moral issues: Human rights, criminal punishment, the legislation of morality, and sexual behavior.]

Hoopes, R. (1980). *The complete peace corps guide.* NY: Dell Publishing Co. [This book goes into detail on practical information relative to challenges and rewards of the Peace Corps life. It discusses how to join the Peace Corps.]

How to get a job in the federal government. (1983). Washington, DC: Superintendent of Documents, U.S. Government Printing Office. [Indicates where and how to apply for jobs with the various federal government agencies.]

Improved career decision making in a changing world. (1991). Garrett Park, MD: Garrett Park Press. [Developed by the National Occupational Information Coordinating Committee this book serves as a guide to sources of career information and provides background for counseling on occupational trends. Trainer's manual also available for this book.]

Jackson, T.F. (1982). *Guerrilla tactics in the job market.* NY: Bantam Books. [Some of the statistics are dated but lists 78 tactics for getting the desired job. Covers the usual areas of resume, interviewing, targeting desired occupation, networking, etc.]

Job search workbook (1991). Detroit: Gale Research Company. [Occupational data and sources of information cited for a number of fields.]

Job Seekers' Guide to Employment. (1988). San Diego, CA: Job Seekers' Publications, P.O. Box 231479, 92123-0910. [Aimed at helping individuals who have been absent from the work force for an extended period. A work book which includes employment forms, selling yourself, researching employer, job search techniques, telephone techniques and interview.]

Kapes*, J.T., & Mastie, M.M. (Eds.). (1988). *A counselor's guide to career assessment instruments.* Alexandria, VA: The National Career Development Association. [Discusses use and interpretation of 43 career assessment instruments. Material was prepared by 62 career counseling professionals.]

Karpati, F.S. (1991). *Lifestyle and career development: A counseling and training workbook.* Hackensack, NJ: Frank Karpati Associates. [This publication is to provide career counselors and human resources professionals a series of career and lifestyle training programs and counseling techniques, exercises, checklists & assessment instruments.]

Kennedy, J.L., & Laramore, D. (1988). *Joyce Lane Kennedy's career book.* Lincolnwood, IL: VGM Career Horizons. [A career book aimed at males and females 15 to 25 years. Subjects covered include positive mind set, types of jobs, professional occupations, personal assessment, career awareness, goals, student jobs, postsecondary education, succeeding on first job.]

Kepner, C.H. & Tregoe, B.B. (1965). *The rational manager: A systematic approach to problem solving & decision making.* NY: McGraw-Hill Book Co. [A structured, objective decision making model that may be used in many applications including career decision making.]

Labowitz, A. & Lea, D. (Eds.). (1986). *Adult career developments: Concepts, issues & practices.* Alexandria, VA: National Career Development Association. [22 chapters and 35 authors who are experts in the career planning and development field discuss all phases of adult career development. Theories, strategies, settings, evaluation, future trends.]

Lathrup, R. (1980). *Don't use a resume.* Berkeley, CA: Ten Speed Press. [Advocates a "qualification brief" rather than the traditional resume. Provides a six page check-off list for providing a qualification brief and contains examples of qualification briefs.]

Laughlin, R.S. (1985). *The job hunter's handbook: A Christian guide.* Waco, TX: Word Book Publishers. [This book is to help you to discover what you do best, identify and understand what organizations will benefit from your presence, establish contact with these organizations and get hired. Discusses Christian living principles. For dedicated Christians.]

Lindquist, C.L. & Miller, D.J. (1990). *Where to start career planning.* Princeton: Peterson's Guides. [An annotated bibliography of books dealing with careers and organized by major occupational groups.]

Looking for employment in foreign countries. (1985). New York: World Trade Academy Press, Inc. [Discusses how to apply for government jobs, religious, non-profit and voluntary organizations, and private enterprises. Contains profiles on 43 countries. Contains sample cover letters and resumes.]

Lovejoy's Career and Vocational Guide. (1990). NY: Simon and Schuster. [Directory of institutions training for job opportunities. Lists professional and trade organizations that will provide information on various occupations. Lists two year postsecondary schools (private and public) that provide majors in various occupations.]

Malloy, J.T. (1975). *Dress for success.* NY: Warner Books. [This book discusses how men should dress for success in the interview and other business and personal situations.]

Malloy, J.T. (1975). *The woman's dress for success book.* NY: Warner Books. [A follow-on book to the "mens" book on proper dressing for women in business and leisure situations.]

Manufacturers directory. (1989-90). Greenville, SC: The Chamber of Commerce. [Lists company name, address, president, phone number, type product and male and female employment for all manufacturing companies in Greenville, SC.]

Martin, P. (1987). *Martins' magic formula for getting the right job.* NY: St. Martin's Press. [Contains advice on changing jobs, changing careers and taking advantage of new employment trends. Covers job hunting tools, prospect file, self assessment, job search, resume, interview, followup, applicant check list, job holder checklist, networking.]

Mason, J. (1987). *Beginnings: a guide to making career choices.* Greenville, SC: Greenville Technical College. [A career planning book for women. Contains information on job search, resume, cover letter, application form and interviewing.]

Mattox, R. (1978). *The Christian employee.* Plainfield, NJ: Logos International. [This book describes seven foundational principles that Christian employees should follow in their work.]

McDaniels, C. (1990). *Developing a professional vita or resume.* Garrett Park, MD: Garrett Park Press. [Describes how to prepare a vita, the key document for persons seeking employment as college teachers.]

Military career guide: Employment and training opportunities in the military. (1988-89). 2500 Green Bay Road, North Chicago, IL 60064. U.S. Military Entrance Processing Command. [Includes detailed information on the various military occupations including the DOT code.]

Miller, G.P. (1978). *After high school.* New York: Cornerstone Library, Inc. [The purpose of this book is to show people how to make well-considered decisions relative to career, life style and marriage by applying and practicing a practical decision-making process.]

Mitchell, J.S. (1982). *I can be anything: A career book for women.* NY: College Entrance Examination Board. [Describes successful professional women in 98 different occupations from airline pilot to osteopathic physician.]

Monthly labor review. (monthly). Washington, DC: United States Department of Labor, Bureau of Labor Statistics. [Projections of the economy, labor force, and occupational change to the year 2000.]

Montross, D.H. & Shinkman, C.J. (Eds.). (1981). *Career development in the 1980s: Theory and practice.* Springfield, IL: Charles C. Thomas Publisher. [Graduate level career counseling text book. The 29 chapters are authored by 32 experts in career counseling.

Myers*, I.B., & McCaulley, M.H. (1985). *Manual: A guide to the development and use of the Myers-Briggs Type Indicator.* Palo Alto, CA: Consulting Psychologists Press. [Detailed information on the MBTI including definition of the 16 types, interpretation, norms, correlations with occupations. If you use the MBTI you need this manual.]

Myers, I.B., & Myers, P.B. (1986). *Gifts differing.* Palo Alto, CA: Consulting Psychologists Press, Inc. [Detailed discussion of the 16 types, an overview of Jung's psychological types theory, effects of preferences on personality, practical implications and dynamics of type development.]

Myers, J.R. & Scott, E.W. (1989). *Getting skilled getting ahead: Your guide for choosing a career and a private career school.* Princeton, NJ: Peterson's Guides. [Discusses jobs available to skilled and unskilled workers, fastest growing applications, salary levels, how to find the appropriate post secondary school, and provides profiles of 119 jobs.]

National survey of professional, administrative, technical, and clerical pay: Private nonservice industries. (March 1988). Washington, DC: United States Department of Labor, Bureau of Labor Statistics. Bulletin 2317. [Summarizes a 1988 salary survey of these workers.]

Occupational outlook handbook*. (1990-91). Washington, DC: United States Department of Labor, Bureau of Labor Statistics. Bulletin 2350. [The authoritative DOL book on several hundred occupations including nature of work, working conditions, employment level, training, advancement, job outlook and earnings.]

Occupational outlook quarterly. Washington, DC: Superintendent of Documents, U.S. Government Printing Office. [This periodical is issued quarterly and describes latest occupational trends, employment outlook, salary levels and occupational descriptions.]

Occupational projections and training data: A statistical and research supplement to the 1990-91 occupational outlook handbook. Washington, DC: United States Department of Labor, Bureau of Labor Statistics. Bulletin 2351. [Provides projections of employment and job opportunities.]

Outlook 2000. (April 1990). Washington, DC: U.S. Department of Labor, Bureau of Labor Statistics. Bulletin 2352. [Presents detailed statistics on economic and employment projections, industry and labor force information for 1976, 1988 and projected to 2000. Also classifies many occupations by projected growth and decline rates.]

Parker, Y. (1988). The resume catalogue: 200 damn good examples. Berkeley: Ten Speed Press. [Examples of resumes for following occupational clusters; management, human resources, administration, finance, accounting. technical, computers, education, therapy, social work, health, marketing, PR, sales and potpourri.]

Peters, T.J., & Waterman, R.J. Jr. (1982). *In search of excellence: Lessons from America's best-run companies.* NY: Harper & Row Publishers. [This book was a best seller. It discusses the secrets to successful business management. It lists eight basic practices characteristic of successfully managed companies.]

Peterson's annual guide to undergraduate study: Four-year colleges. (1991). Princeton, NJ: Peterson's Guides. [Provides detailed information on four year colleges in the U.S.]

Peterson's two-year colleges. (1990). Princeton, NJ: Peterson's Guides. [Contains detailed information on the two year accredited colleges in the U.S.]

Professional careers sourcebook: An information guide for career planning. (1990). Detroit: Gale Research Company. [Cites books, associations, newsletters, employment services, and other references for a number of career fields.]

Sheehy, G. (1979). *Passages; Predictable crises of adult life.* NY: Bantam Books. [The best selling book that describes predictable crises that men and women go through. The steps are the same for both sexes but the developmental rhythms are not.]

Smith, D.C. (1990). *Great careers; The fourth of july guide to careers, internships, and volunteer opportunities in the non-profit sector.* Garrett Park, MD: Garrett Park Press. [Written by 40 college career counseling directors, cites hundreds of organizations and publications dealing with nonprofit employment].

South Carolina industrial directory. (1990). Columbia, SC: South Carolina State Development Board. [Lists all South Carolina industrial companies alphabetically by county. Provides company name, address, telephone number, CEO, number of employees and products.]

South Carolina job search assistance guide. (1986). Columbia, SC: SC Employment Security Commission. [A discussion of South Carolina's shifting job market, economic and employment situation. One chapter is entitled "Job Hunting in the Palmetto State." Lists 42 state licensing Boards for various professional occupations.]

South Carolina job search assistance guide. (1989). Columbia, SC: South Carolina Employment Security Commission. [Provides information on living and working in South Carolina. Covers all types of industrial, trade and service industries. Also discusses career planning, job search techniques, resumes, interviews, and time management.]

South Carolina labor market information directory. (1988). Columbia, SC: South Carolina Employment Security Commission. [Lists various publications in South Carolina which provide information relative to labor and employment.]

Starting out: Experts' guide to success. Salt Lake City, UT: American Express Travel Related Services Co., Inc., P.O. Box 31560. [Written for the student who is about to enter the work force. Includes information on career planning and goal-setting, and how to advance his/her career.]

Staton, T.F., (1982). *How to study.* Nashville, TN: Thomas F. Staton, P.O. Box 40273, ZIP 37204. [Short term memory, long term memory, and PQRST study method (preview, question, read, state and test), listening to a lecture, psychological factors influencing learning, class discussions and exams.]

Story, W.D. (1976). *Career Dimensions I: An exposure to life planning and an approach for developing a personal framework for career planning.* Crotonville, NY: General Electric Co. [The first of four workbooks developed to assist G.E. management personnel to select meaningful life goals and to accomplish his/her next career development actions.]

Story, W.D. (1976). *Career Dimensions II: An approach & some tools to help you think & plan realistically for your future, growth, & career.* Crotonville, NY: General Electric Co. [Contains 13 "action" exercises requiring about 14 hours of time. They include such activities as prediction grid, career realities, feedback interview, bridging, etc.]

Story, W.D. (1976). *Career Dimensions III: A how-to-do-it guide for the manager to use in coaching employees about their careers & dealing with tough questions & messages.* Crotonville, NY: General Electric Co. [Eight rules for dealing with career planning and development of employees, how to approach employees in "lay off" situations, and career discussions.]

Story, W.D. (1976). *Career Dimensions IV: A handbook for professionals in employee relations & training & development to use in implementing realistic career planning with clients.* Crotonville, NY: General Electric Co. [Importance of career planning, how to generate interest in career planning, methodology of personal career planning.]

Strategies for study. (1982). Logan, IA: The Perfection Form Co. [A workbook for use with school children who are having difficulty in studying.]

The career development quarterly. (1991). Alexandria, VA: National Career Development Association. [A scholarly journal discuss-

140

ing all types of career counseling issues.]

The college handbook. (1991). NY: Guidance Publishing, The College Board. [Information on two year and four year colleges in the U.S. including majors, costs, enrollment, etc.]

The jobseeker: A source book for youth in NY state. (1980). Albany, NY: New York State Dept. of Labor. [The book is written for youth who have recently entered or are about to enter the New York State job market. It includes resume, interviewing, job search, where to get more information about jobs and 122 job profiles.]

Walker, L.H., Tague-Smith, S., VanDerhoff, L., Earley, C. (1983). *A self-assessment and self-planning manual.* Albany, NY: Regents External Degree Program, Cultural Education Center, Room 5D45. [A workbook for people considering going to college in the New York State Regents External Degree Program.]

Weinrach, S.G. (1979). *Career counseling: Theoretical and practical perspectives.* NY: McGraw-Hill. [A graduate level text for career counseling. The sections of the text are the counselor and society, structural approaches, process approaches, special treatment groups, and counseling across the life span.]

Working for yourself: Career planning information. (1988). Eugene, OR: National Career Information System, 1787 Agate St. [Discusses things to be considered in starting a business. Includes the Entrepreneur's Quiz which indicates how the person taking the A.I. compares to a norming sample of successful entrepreneurs.]

Working Woman. New York: Working Woman. [A monthly magazine aimed at professional and business women. Provides suggestions on how women can get the desired job and advance in their careers].

Wright*, J.W., & Dwyer, E.J. (1990). *The American almanac of jobs and salaries.* New York: Avon Books. [A detailed discussion of hundreds of jobs including salary levels and projected employment increases to the year 2010.]

Zunker, V.G. (1990). *Career Counseling.* Pacific Grove, CA: Brooks/Cole Publishing Company. [Career counseling text for college graduate program.]